FISHING
for
SOULS

FISHING
for
SOULS

Ottomar E. Bickel

Illustrated by Susan B. Crawford

Roller Coaster Press
St. Paul, Minnesota

Published by Roller Coaster Press.
  1167 Ryan Avenue W., Minnesota 55113-5929
  Tel. 888-894-1594
  E-mail: pmbickel@aol.com

© 2000 by Roller Coaster Press, all rights reserved

Permission is hereby granted for churches and parachurch organizations to copy individual items in this book free of charge for use in not-for-profit publications such as worship bulletins, song books, and newsletters, provided this notation is appended:
  From *Fishing for Souls*, by Ottomar E. Bickel,
  (© 2000 Roller Coaster Press, Tel. 888-894-1594).

For all other uses, no part of this book may be reproduced or transmitted in any form or by any means, electronic or mechanical, including photocopying, recording or by any information storage and retrieval system, without written permission from the publisher, except for the inclusion of brief quotes in a review.

Unless otherwise noted, Scripture quotations taken from the HOLY BIBLE, NEW INTERNATIONAL VERSION. Copyright © 1973, 1978, 1984 by International Bible Society.

Cover design and illustrations by Susan B. Crawford.

Library of Congress Catalog Card Number: 99-900554

ISBN 0-9663765-1-X

Subjects: 1. Evangelistic work.
          2. Christian devotional material.
          3. Hymnody.

CONTENTS

Chapter 1 Let's Go Fishing! 11
    Learning from the Master   11
    The Biggest Fish Story Ever   13
    A Tip for Fishers of Men   14
    Very Personal   15
    We Have a Neat God   16
    Holy Love   17
    Witnessing May Take a Lifetime   18
    Prisoner of War   22

Chapter 2 Christ's Influence 23
    Come, Pilgrim, Walk with Me   23
    Hear the Music in the Music of Christmas   24
    Our Christmas Hope   25
    What Is Jesus Like?   26
    Sunrise Sonrise   27
    A Palm Sunday Psalm   28
    Behold, the Goat of God   29
    What Jesus Dreaded Most   30
    Always the Same   31
    The White and Gold Lily   32
    Easter—A New Dawn   33
    Miracles! Miracles! Miracles!   34
    Jesus Does the Laundry   34
    Poetry Defined   35
    Jesus Is the Key   36
    Who Is the Rock   38
    New Verse to "His Name Is Wonderful"   38

Chapter 3 How to Be Saved 39
    Guard against the Interceptor   39
    New Verse for "You'll Never Walk Alone"   40
    Whom Does God Choose?   41
    Come!   42
    Blood Cleanser   43
    The Names of Our Peace   44

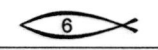

What Can Match Christ's Resurrection?   45
Life Billboards   46
He Is Our Life   48
What Grade Would You Give Jesus?   50

Chapter 4 Life in the Spirit   51
Christmas Mystery   51
The First Shall Be Last   52
Continual Baptism   52
Finders, Keepers   53
Bible Marking System   54
Gifts Are for Sharing   56
Second Wind for the Christian Walk   57
Like a Drop of Water   58
Words in Tune   59
How to Set a Church on Fire   60
Martin Luther Describes the Soul-Winner   62

Chapter 5 Sharing Good News   63
The First Thing on Jesus' Mind   63
Every Soul Is Precious   64
Witnessing in the Spirit   65
A Short and Sweet Story   66
A Soul-Winner's Prayer   67
Caught by the Wrist   68
Normal Christian Lifestyle   69
I Must Speak   70
"Evangelical" Is Our Middle Name   71
Freeze!   72
Ignition   73
Guide to the Soul-Winner   74
The Parachute   75
Are You a Good Egg?   76
The Key of Life   77
Where Would I Go?   79
Improving Fishing Skills   80
A Letter to Billy Graham   83
Sweet Harvest   84

Chapter 6 Devotional Life   85
Tested, Tempered, Triumphant   85
Prayer for a Worshipful Spirit   86
Jesus, Rapture of My Heart   87
Holy Land Morning   88

With Jesus by the Sea   89
God Be with You Till We Meet Again   90
Only Jesus   91
Needed: Prayer Warriors   92
Praise God   93
For Deep Thirst   93
How Deep Is the Ocean?   94
O Lord, What a Morning!   94
The Lamb Is My Shepherd   96
In Sync with God   98
What I See by the Sea   99
Reason to Follow   100

Chapter 7 Family and Nation 101
A Wedding Benediction   101
Marvelous Marriage Mathematics   102
Like Two Left Feet   103
Precious Appreciation   103
Love that Never Fails   104
You'll See Adam before I Will   105
Prayer for the Family   106
His Banner over Us Is Love   107
Primary Election   108
The Closing of the American Mind   109
Civil War II   110
There Is a Way, America   111

Chapter 8 Heaven, Our Home 113
Nearer Home   113
The Agony and Ecstasy of Aging   114
Augusta Vedra   116
Fountain of Youth   117
The Rock of Ages Hall of Fame   118
Thoughts of Heaven   119
Family Forerunner   120
The Soul of This Child   121
Our Comfort, Our Home in Heaven   121
My Lifetime Fishing Buddy   122
What Good Would Heaven Be without God?   123
Eternal Attention   124

Titles Listed Alphabetically 125

Scripture Index 126

ACKNOWLEDGEMENTS

This book has been a family affair. Heartfelt thanks go to:
- Karla and Terry Whitsitt, my daughter and son-in-law, for a thousand editorial and secretarial tasks.
- Daughter Susan Crawford for art, calligraphy, and layout editing.
- Son Philip Bickel for editing, typesetting, and publishing.
- Daughter Eunice Hester for legal advice.
- Wife Ruth-Esther Hillila-Bickel for editing, musical arrangements, and encouragement.
- Granddaughter Sarah Klein for secretarial tasks.

This book is also a Zion family affair. In particular I wish to thank:
- Co-pastors Kent Wendorf and Jim Zinkowich for their love, prayers and encouragement.
- Secretaries Lillian Henkel, Joan Bevan, Carol Sippola, Carol Lageson, and Jan Brown for their cheerful, sanctified service.
- Every person with whom I have shared the Word of God over the years.

I also wish to acknowledge the scores of friends whose pre-publication purchases of this book funded its production.

You have all been valuable contributors to my life's work and to this volume. Thank you!

Ottomar E. Bickel

EDITOR'S FOREWORD

Pastor Ottomar Bickel, my father, served in the pastoral ministry for fifty-three years. Living in northeastern Ohio, he learned about maple sugar. To produce this delicacy, you must collect many gallons of maple sap, boil them for hours until you get a small amount of syrup, and then boil the syrup for hours longer, until you have a tiny—but delicious—portion of maple sugar.

This book is the maple sugar of Dad's ministry. In it you will find condensed the choicest insights from preparing thousands of sermons, writing hundreds of evangelistic radio programs, and witnessing about Christ to thousands of individuals looking for the purpose and meaning of life.

Dad is a communicator. His sermons regularly include picture language and stories which speak to children and adults alike. Dad's love for Jesus is evident and contagious. Some preachers merely refer to the Gospel, assuming their listeners already know the details. Dad avoided that mistake. He found joy in relating the details. Whenever he discovered a new way to explain Christ to people, he was eager to inform me about it. I freely admit I borrowed his ideas often.

Dad is the best one-on-one personal witness I know. He has been the Holy Spirit's midwife at hundreds of new births. Faithfully serving one church for forty-eight years, his perseverance paid off. In many cases, people to whom he had witnessed decades earlier returned asking him, "I know I failed to listen back then. But would you please explain that message of hope to me again?" He was always thrilled to do so.

Editing Dad's material has been sweet for my soul, like maple sugar. May this book bless you as it has blessed me.

In the service of the King of kings,
Philip M. Bickel

In Memoriam

In loving memory of
my wife Ruth Kathryn,
my parents Lydia and Fred,
my brothers Victor and Lester,
my in-laws, Clara, Frank Sr.,
Frank Jr., Lois, and Harold,
and all the rest of my dear family and friends
who are already safe in heaven with Jesus!

Dedication

This book is dedicated with love
to my wife Ruth-Esther,
to my children and grandchildren,
to all my brothers and sisters in the Lord,
to those still not caught by His love,
and most of all to my Savior and Lord,
Jesus Christ.

Let's Go Fishing!

Learning from the Master

A popular bumper sticker declares: "I'd rather be fishing!" When I read that motto, I realize how fortunate I am that my whole life is taken up with fishing, one way or another. You see, my hobby is fishing for fish. My vocation is fishing for souls. And my spiritual hobby is personal soul-winning.

To Jesus, fishing came first and last. He went fishing every day of His three years of ministry, because He wanted to draw all people to Himself. He called His disciples from their nets to become fishers of men and women. Christ's ministry took place mostly outdoors. His life and preaching were plain and simple. If He had had an office, there would have always been a sign hung on the door: GONE FISHING!

My experience. When I was a young pastor in Michigan, I often spent my days off with my friend, Pastor Fred Wiese, fishing in the Manistee River. It was my first experience trout fishing. Often I was skunked, meaning I caught only small fish. Meanwhile, Pastor Wiese caught big ones. I assumed he was just lucky. He coached me how to catch bigger fish, but at first I didn't pay attention. Eventually, I took his advice, imitated everything he did, and even studied trout fishing books on my own. After years of carefully learning effective angling skills, I became a seasoned fisherman. Since then my children, grandchildren, and other young people have fished with me. Whenever any of them became frustrated over their small catches, I tried to teach them what I had learned.

My friend, Pastor Wiese, also coached me how to catch men. He modeled for me how to make calls and how to reach people. Later in my ministry, I learned from: evangelist Billy Graham; James Kennedy of Evangelism Explosion; Francis Schaeffer, minister to youth and intellectuals; Herb Franz and Bob Griffin of Lutheran Evangelism Movement; Dawson Trotman of the Navigators; Bill Bright and Josh McDowell of Campus Crusade for Christ. They and others taught me how to train people to catch souls.

The purpose of this book. I want to tell you about my Best Friend and Best Fishing Buddy, my Savior and Lord Jesus Christ. I also want to pass on to you some of the effective soul-catching skills He has taught me through the years. Reaching people is a process of growth with all Christians. We are all at a certain point in skill development, and we all can learn to do better. Athletes need practice, but some Christians seem to think they can be soul-winners without practice. Although Peter, Andrew, James, and John were expert fishermen, to become fishers of people they needed years of walking with Jesus and being tutored by Him.

Jesus was unique. He sat in a boat to preach. His voice echoed off the water to the ears and hearts of the crowd. However, He did not always talk to great crowds. He did much personal work too. All His life on earth He was catching individuals. He had personal dialogues with Zacchaeus, Nicodemus, the woman at the well, Mary, Martha, and their brother Lazarus, also little children and their parents, the thief on the cross, and Peter, when He asked him three times, "Do you love Me?"

Just as you don't land every fish you hook, not everyone believed Jesus. Judas squirmed out of the net. King Herod played with Him as a toy. Pilate asked many questions, but did not listen to Jesus' answers. The High Priests, supposedly in tune with God, turned a deaf ear. But still Christ continued to love them and all of us who bear the title "sinner." It is impossible for Jesus to love us only a little.

In all the Lord's personal ministry He modeled how He intended to love and work with people—not by whip cracking and keeping in line—but by embracing, making peace, rebuilding, and repairing. Jesus truly "dwelt among us." He never said, "Come only during office hours." He loved everyone in particular and no one in general. He treated with great tenderness everyone seeking Him. When the people followed Him around the lake, He saw them as sheep without a shepherd. So He sat down and talked with them, even though He was very tired.

Jesus is the Lover of Souls. He is the Master Fisherman, because He brings people out of death to life. Jesus is still calling His disciples. He is calling us to be fishers of the men, women, and children He loves so much that He died for them, as well as for you and me! When fish are caught, they die and are eaten. But when souls are caught by Jesus' love, they are raised from death to life. So get your line into the water and your net ready!

THE BIGGEST FISH STORY EVER

The apostle Peter is often called the Big Fisherman. Peter and his partners, Andrew, James, John, and Zebedee, were real fishermen. No city-softies out on a fishing weekend, who sometimes don't even clean and eat their fish, but bury them in the garden. Peter and his buddies were commercial fisherman. They had hard callouses from handling the oars, sails, and nets. They had scars from thousands of bristling fins and from the sharp knives with which they cleaned the fish.

Peter and the others endured bad weather, griped about catchless nights, cursed torn nets, quarreled with other fishermen over choice fishing spots. Peter barked at his wife when she moaned about lean times. He envied others who seemed to have an easier way to make a living.

Yes, like us all, Peter had open sins and hidden sins of the heart. How do we know? One beautiful morning Jesus stood in Peter's boat and preached. Peter and his fishing buddies heard about God's love and holiness. Then they obeyed Christ's strange order to put out their nets in midday. When they hauled in so many fish that the nets were tearing, Peter knew this was bigger than any fish story he had ever heard or told.

Amid the excitement, Peter recognized the presence of Divine majesty in Christ and sensed his own moral failures, like laymen often do when ministers are present. Peter became as self-conscious as a fisherman who, dressed in his grubby clothes, happens to enter a room filled with nicely dressed people. In the presence of Christ's holiness, Peter remembered all his sins and said, "Go away from me, Lord; I am a sinful man" (Lk. 5:8). But Jesus came to save sinners. He taught Peter and the others that all things are possible to those who believe, even the cleansing of a sinner.

So, Peter was saved by faith in the blood of Christ's sacrifice. And as Peter followed Jesus, the Lord's prediction came true: "Don't be afraid; from now on you will catch men" (Lk. 5:10).

A Tip for Fishers of Men

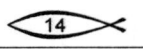

A boy a-fishing went one day,
 a country boy with country ways;
  who loved to fish away his days
 by sparkling streams in solitude
  that always seemed to lift his mood.

The stream meandered through the ranch:
 an alder bush grew by its banks.
  He cut and trimmed a slender branch,
 tied on a length of store-bought string
  complete with well-bent safety pin.

HE MUST INCREASE BUT I MUST DECREASE. JOHN 3:30

As he began to fish that morn,
 a man went by him, city-born;
  observed his crude device with scorn,
 for he was smartly fitted out
  with rod and gear to catch the trout.

Late in the day the city man
 returned that way with empty hand,
  only to see upon the sand
 a stringer full of bright-hued trout
  caught by the clumsy country lout.

"You caught all those? I had one bite!"
 The boy replied, "Stay out of sight
  when you fish trout, don't block the light
 Your shadow frightens fish away,
  that's why your creel's so light today."

Now take this tip, you who fish men—
 to do the opposite to them;
  to raise from death to life again
 keep your SELF out of sight, be sure
  show only Jesus, He's the lure.

Very Personal

God says, "I have loved you with an everlasting love; I have drawn you with loving-kindness." Jeremiah 31:3
I know the plans I have for you, plans to prosper you and not to harm you, plans to give you hope and a future. Jeremiah 29:11

These verses from Jeremiah are two of my favorite love notes from God. Why? Because they are so personal. I have met many people who doubt they can know God personally. But God is a person and He is personal. He names Himself the "I Am." He is much more than a force. He is a person with character, identity and personality. He thinks about us and plans for us, hurts with us and cares about us. He has a personal interest in us.

God says, "Fear not, for I have redeemed you; I have summoned you by name; you are mine" (Is. 43:1). He claims personal ownership. We belong to Him. We need not fear that He will selfishly smother us with His great love or simply toy with us for a time. He loves us truly. He loves us permanently. He gave His Son as a cross-ransom for our sins. He gives us a name—His own—and claims us as His very children.

The Bible is the mail box we can open daily to receive a personal letter from the Lord, filled with assuring hugs of forgiveness when we repent, protective warnings for our day, maps for our way, medicine for our ills, and comfort for our hearts.

Here is one of the Lord's love letters to you: "So do not fear, for I am with you; do not be dismayed, for I am your God. I will strengthen you and help you; I will uphold you with my righteous right hand" (Is. 41:10). His right hand is Jesus.

The Lord is not aloof. He does not play hard to get. James says, "Draw near to God and God will draw near to you" (4:8). He is truly a friend. He chose us. He called us and won us back to Himself. He wept over Jerusalem when they rejected His friendship. He grieves over the slightest coolness on our part. If you do not have a close, personal relationship with God, whose fault is it?

Here is how personal He is: Place your own name in the blank spaces below. Make this precious promise personal and keep it personal.

"For God so loved _____, that he gave His only Son, that _____, who believes in Him, shall not perish, but have eternal life" (Jn. 3:16).

We Have a Neat God

Recently, I heard some teenagers exclaim, "Neat!" in response to something they found remarkable. Although the word *neat* is used a lot these days, I cannot recall anywhere in the Bible, in religious literature, or in Christian music where God is called neat.

My dictionary lists eight definitions for neat. As I reflected on them, I realized they describe the Lord perfectly.

1. Neat: clean and in order. The Lord is holy, clean, unspotted by any evil. He created the world with order and declared, "It is very good [neat]!"
2. Neat: able and willing to keep things in order. While our lives may fall apart, He is busy restoring order and purpose to our days.
3. Neat: well-formed, in proportion. God is not lopsided. He is balanced in His love for us and His correction of our sins.
4. Neat: skillful, clever. What does it take to make a universe and keep it running? The very highest intelligence, creativity, and integrity.
5. Neat: nothing mixed in, undiluted. God is complete in Himself. He seeks no additive and needs no additive. Though He does not need us, He chooses to love us.
6. Neat: (slang) very pleasing, fine, most enjoyable. Great is the Lord and worthy of praise! He's in a class by Himself. Those who know Him always find joy in Him.
7. Neat: clear, net profit. Paul said, "We are complete in Christ" (Col. 2:20). We lose nothing—ever—by sticking to Him. Everything about Him is gain.
8. Neaten: to clean, order, arrange. First, God neatens our souls, removing the stain of sin. Then He sends us out to share the Gospel, a message which the Holy Spirit uses to tidy up the lives of others, until the whole world is neatened.

Even the Latin words for *neat* are thoroughly appropriate for God. The Latin noun, *nitidus*, means gleaming, and the Latin verb, *nitere*, means to shine. John said, "God is light; and in Him there is no darkness at all" (1 Jn. 1:5). Jesus said, "I am the light of the world. Whoever follows me will never walk in darkness, but will have the light of life" (Jn. 8:12).

I can't help but wonder why neat had never been used to describe God before. After all, He is neater than anyone else, and what He does is neater than anything else that has been done. No matter which definition we use, we have a neat God!

Holy Love

"God is love." 1 John 4:7
"You alone are holy." Revelation 15:4

Snowscape whiteness,
Reflected brightness
Dazzles our eyes;
Near snow blindness
Threat'ning darkness.
So holy is God!

New-snow softness,
Lamb of God whiteness
Covers our sins;
Full forgiveness,
Blood-bought pureness.
So loving is God!

True perfection,
Pure loving-kindness,
Merge as one;
His compassion
Matches His justness.
So gracious is God!

Witnessing May Take a Lifetime

A fisherman must be patient. Fishers of lost people must also be patient. You will yet catch your limit, if you do not give up. It may even take a lifetime. I found out.

Since I served in one parish area during five decades I got to see several slow-motion miracles of conversion after many years of fishing.

Frank. The first story is fitting because this friend was a fisherman. I met Frank at a wedding reception. As we talked about various subjects, he let me know that "church" was not for him! However, we hit it off on fishing. In fact, he invited me to share his boat on Pymatuning Reservoir, forty miles east. We soon had four bobbers floating on the water, two for each of us.

The walleye pike were ignoring our bait. I got impatient. So I thought I would impress my new friend with my fly casting skill and rigged up my fly rod. After a few minutes my new buddy, Frank, showed me one of his finest traits, frankness.

He asked, "What are you going to say to the game warden when he shows up and sees your three fishing rods? The law says two is the limit."

Over the next thirty-five years, Frank often delighted in telling this story to others, especially when I was present. While Frank chuckled, he also saw my embarrassment and my penitence. I prayed that sooner or later he would allow me into his "inner sanctum" and allow me to discuss his need of a relationship with God. I wedged my foot in the door a number of times at weddings, funerals, and other occasions. In addition, his sister-in-law often invited him to church.

Meanwhile Frank and his wife, Dorothy, prospered and built a home in the country, offering gracious hospitality. My family often enjoyed use of their farm pond filled with bluegill and bass. We even caught an occasional trout, much appreciated.

At a much later date, my fishing buddy met up with his doctors concerning a troublesome ailment, which turned out to be cancer. When the doctor declared the unhappy diagnosis, I called on Frank at the hospital and later at home. He was cheerful despite the prognosis.

This was not the only time I had shared the Gospel with him, but it now appeared to comfort him. He also was willing to hear his sister-in-law's testimony after brushing it aside for twelve years as "feminine immaturity."

She brought to Frank a cassette I had made with hymns and brief messages on the promises of God. The tape captured his attention, for he invited friends and relatives to listen to it. As his condition grew more serious and threatening, the recording cradled his mind with divine light and peace.

As I often called on Frank at his home, we would watch the birds feed at his window and tell stories of the past, but also we would frankly gaze into the future. The light of this life grew more dim, but hope from God's Word grew brighter. I saw how Frank drew strength from the Savior whom we now shared. So also his family and visitors found courage, because Frank was full of peace and hope in the risen Christ.

The Scriptures from my "technicolor" Bible (See pp. 54.) had interested him, to understand the reasons for underlining verses in various colors. Now his Bible lay open on the table. Also I would respond to his song requests for him and family members to hear.

About three weeks after I had begun to call, he visibly began to slip. One evening as I was about to leave, Frank said, "I think it's today!"

I asked, "Do you mean God is going to take you home?"

"Yes!" he replied.

So I sat down and we scoured the Scriptures, rejoicing over his prospects. The next morning at 8 o'clock God chose to take my fishing buddy home to be with his Savior.

George. That is not my only thirty-five year story of patient witnessing. George was married to a lovely woman named Sophie, a member of my church. He often graciously welcomed my family and me into his home for a meal and an evening of Ping-Pong. He was a successful businessman but rarely attended church.

When God finally got through to George, He again used music, as well as a nervous disorder which George and I had both experienced. Because of a yen to be a musician, George purchased a home organ which he often played. He then insisted on taping me singing some hymns for him and Sophie to enjoy later.

George was in and out of the hospital for stress-related stomach problems, a malady which God used to prepare his heart. One night his wife called me. This was about a year before he came to Christ. Sophie explained that George had insomnia and that she had sat up with him for three nights, so I went over in the evening.

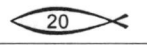

After visiting downstairs, I said, "George, this not sleeping is no good. Let us help you to bed. Sophie can get you ready and then I'll come up. We'll talk a while as we have down here." As I sat by his bed we kidded a little, because George always laughed and kidded (he tried never to be unhappy!) Then I quietly sang "Blessed Assurance" and other songs. Soon George was asleep.

A year later he had not yet received Christ, but then—to our amazement and God's glory—he changed in two days! It occurred during yet another hospital stay. During one visit he had looked right through me as I shared the Gospel, but the next day someone gave him a tract to read. He called me to the hospital and asked me excitedly, "Is this what you mean?" The tract began, "I know I am a sinner and I can't save myself."

This time as we went over the Gospel, George's face shone as the light of Christ dawned upon him. He joined the church thirty-five years after I first called on him in 1947. He no longer sat on the sidelines! He never missed church, and he prayed enthusiastically for the Lord's work.

What prepared George to receive the message of God's redemptive love for sinners? The love and prayers of his wife along with my friendship evangelism.

John. John was a good man, an elder in a church which stressed good works. We met when I approached him about buying a parcel of land where I intended to build a cabin. We hit it off immediately. But he never sold me the land. Instead, he graciously leased me an acre for twenty years at the price of $1 per annum.

In the ensuing years, we often discussed the God of the Scriptures. Years later, he had a severe heart attack. He called me to visit him in the hospital the night before surgery. He was comforted to know his certainty of going to heaven if and when he would die was not based on his many good deeds. John expressed his awareness of his sinful human nature despite years of good deeds and trying to obey God's laws. We agreed that night that God's acceptance of us was based on Christ's sacrifice on the cross on our behalf.

John did not survive that illness. The surgery did not save him. But Christ did!

More examples. Sometimes it is not as easy, such as when we don't have common interests. There was one man whom I visited often over several years. He would discuss many books and articles he had read, giving the impression he did not need to know about God. In later years when he was facing death, this man prayed the sinner's prayer with a young assistant pastor.

Previously, this aging father would complain to the young pastor, "All Pastor Bickel ever talks about is Jesus." When I heard this, I chuckled, thinking of all those conversations we had over the years about topics and books he had chosen. Sometimes it may take much patient listening and speaking only a few words about Christ before a person is ready to listen to the Spirit's call.

Although it may take patience, still there is a two-sided blessing as we seek to help people and share God's love over the years. They often teach us something and gladly help us as they give in return. I experienced this kind of joy in waiting for God to bear fruit in my fellow carpenter and friend, Paul, who helped me with several projects to improve my home. And there was the college girl who asked, "How can God love us that much?" We learn a lot as people ask their questions.

Other means. God uses even our frailties and weaknesses to prepare us as His witnesses. I once had a nervous condition which incapacitated me for a year. Many people prayed for me. Finally, I found help for this condition and was able to return to work. But that was not a wasted year at all. Over the following years, the Lord sent me about 180 people who were troubled by the same condition. Many of them I was able to lead to Christ as I shared with them the methods which had brought me healing.

And of course, the Lord uses every member in the Body of Christ to reach people. I have seen Him use faithful church members to come alongside and visit those who are ill or dying. One man developed cancer and then came to trust Christ when a friend brought a sermon tape to hear. They sat and listened, along with the man's wife, who had prayed for her husband for twenty years. What a joy to be part of the process of God leading His lost children home.

May you see from these stories that the Lord is able to soften hearts. We can expect various reactions to our witness, our "fishing." But leave your line in the water and don't give up. The Lord is faithful! As we prayerfully wait and trust in Him, He surely will lead others to receive His gracious and patient love.

Prisoner of War

In some cases, we will not learn the results of our witness until we reach heaven. Such is the case with Walter.

I met him in an unusual setting. In 1942, I was one of several pastors asked by the United States government to minister to German soldiers at a nearby prisoner of war camp. During the day, the six hundred POWs worked in the orchards and fields of western Michigan. During the evening, they had a lot of time to think about the state of the world and the state of their own hearts. They wondered about their future. They worried about their families. Since they were treated with kindness at the camp and in the nearby farms, they questioned their political loyaties.

Every Monday evening for six months, I held an informal worship service in a field tent. Fifty to seventy-five of them would attend. I preached in German, and we sang familiar German hymns from memory. Walter Friedman, a German officer in the camp, was assigned to be my translator. Since I already knew German, his main task was to help clarify my intentions.

I once brought the prisoners some art materials to augment their supply. A while later, they exhibited their art work in a variety of media. Walter's items were quite well done.

After each service, Walter and five others would remain for a discussion, sometimes lasting several hours. We focused on the topics people are supposed to avoid: religion and politics. Their questions revealed a spiritual probing, a search for truth, and the longing for a foundation for their lives. Our conversations were always amicable, and we established mutual trust. Munching on refreshments and listening to classical records added to the informality and warmth. I once asked the American officer in charge whether he thought these talks might be considered politically "dangerous." He assured me there was no problem.

After the war, Walter settled down in Tübingen, Germany and got married. Our friendship continued through sporadic correspondence. Thirty years later, when Ruth and I began to tour Europe periodically, we visited Walter and his wife every two or three years—five visits in all. Thus a four-way friendship developed. Walter asked many questions about God and the Bible, and I told him how to pray to receive Christ. He never did so in my presence, but I hope and trust that he did, since he had a seeking heart.

2

CHRIST'S INFLUENCE

COME, PILGRIM, WALK WITH ME

Come with me to Galilee; see all my green hills of home.
Along that shore I'll teach you more—the full meaning of shalom.

Come let's go to Jericho by the old wilderness way.
Let us with Zacchaeus dine and see him changed in a day.

Watch with me in Gethsemane, my olive grove of prayer.
Hear my cry, ponder why I knew such fear and despair.

Climb with me to Calvary; relive again those hard hours.
True review will renew your spiritual powers.

Stroll with me in victory, in the Garden of the Tomb;
Let me start to teach your heart life in the uppermost room.

Make it three who share with me along the Emmaus way.
As you learn, your heart will burn, you'll know it's me when I pray.

Shield your eyes where proud Saul dies on the Damascus road.
Then, like Paul, you too tell all why I was crucified.

Come fish with me on Galilee seeking the lost and wayward.
To all the earth, bring new birth by My life-giving word.

Then rise with me to the heavenly; by faith you're as good as there.
Feast your eyes on Paradise, of which you are joint heir.

Hear the Music in the Music of Christmas

The chimes play "Silent Night, Holy Night." Who does not know that melody? The organ plays "O Come, All Ye Faithful". We all know that's Christmas music. It comes and goes with the season. It's welcome and pleasant to the ear. It invites emotions and nostalgia. But is that all?

Do you hear the music in the music? Do you hear the melody in the melodies—the melody of hope? Without God, we are hollow people, filled only with elusive, self-pleasing dreams that never really come true. Some settle for too little at Christmas, even though this holy day can begin a whole new life.

One Christmas season, my two calling partners and I visited a family that had started to attend our church. The parents and three children greeted us warmly. Gifts sat under a brightly decorated tree. A fire crackled in the fireplace. Christmas music played in the background. With so many signs of readiness for the celebration of Christmas, we could have assumed this family was prepared for the festival.

However, we took the opportunity to present the Gospel plan of salvation, because it alone is the basis of Christmas hope. Amid all the decorations, God was offering this family more than a festival. The parents expressed the desire to receive Christ personally. They and the children, ages eight, eleven, and fourteen, prayed the repentant sinner's prayer, trusted in Jesus as their Savior, and turned their lives over to God's direction.

A year later the father of this now Christian family, helped with Christmas preparations at our church. As we looked at the decorated church, he said to me, "This is my first real Christmas. The ones before were hollow compared to this."

Now he heard the music in the music: The love of Jesus who came to our rescue. Now he heard the melody in the melodies: Jesus came to redeem me and all people. Finally, he knew the real joy of Christmas, true peace with God through Jesus Christ.

> Silent night! Holy night!
> All our fears, put to flight.
> Christ has come to set us free
> That by faith we all may be
> Heirs of heavenly peace,
> Heirs of heavenly peace.

CHRIST'S INFLUENCE 25

OUR CHRISTMAS HOPE

1. Our Christmas hope is full and bright and glor-i-ous, It qui-ets hearts with gen-tle touch di-vine. The Christ child is a gift e-ter-nal for us, Which we, like Mar-y, treasure in our mind.
2. Man first was like his ho-ly heaven-ly Fa-ther; Then lost it all in greed-y lust for more. God gave His Son, His high-est, gold-en treasure To be melt down and poured in-to our form.
3. His worth was more than all our worth to-ge-ther; His life as ran-som for our souls was paid. From bank-rupt state we rise to wealth for-ev-er, As soon as we will bend to take His aid.
4. Our Christmas joy is not a one day plea-sure, Not quick-ly gone when lights no long-er glow; A last-ing good, im-pos-si-ble to meas-ure, Our scar-let sin-stains now as white as snow.
5. Our Christmas praise pours out in song and mu-sic, A-round the world takes man-y forms and tones. Lord, tune our hearts and rhyme us with Your Spir-it, That, pen-i-tent, we trust in Christ a-lone.

Our God is good, so ver-y good.

Text: Ottomar E. Bickel, 1976
Tune: O sälla land 11 10 11 10

And Mary said, "My soul doth magnify the Lord, and my spirit hath rejoiced in God my Saviour." Luke 1:46–47

What Jesus Is Like

Precious as gold
Pure as silver
Heart-warming as the sun
Enchanting as a star
Is Jesus

Dazzling as a diamond
Spirit-lifting as a rainbow
Delightful as a daffodil
Awesome as a rugged mountain
Is Jesus

Winsome as a child
Tender as a mother
Caring as a father
Welcome as a true friend
Is Jesus

Comforting as a psalm
Refreshing as a spring
Satisfying as fresh bread
Inspiring as a hymn
Is Jesus

Burdened for the lost
Determined to save
True to His Word
Conqueror of the grave
Is Jesus

Solid as a rock
Strong as a fortress
Complete as a circle
More than enough
For all our sins
Is Jesus!

SUNRISE

The rising sun comes, full of promise,
Friend of day and foe of night.

Circumnavigator of the globe,
Wonder worker of the Lord.

Scaler of every mountain height,
Searcher of the ocean depth.

Welcome guest in every clime,
Joy to all the ships at sea.

Ancient time piece of the day,
Wake-up call to all who sleep.

Supplier of all green and growth,
Dispenser of life's nourishment.

Makes each day a new beginning,
A fresh start for soul and body.

Prayer-bell for all God's children,
Beacon of the coming Savior.

Warming hearts & healing hurts,
Lamp to our feet, light to our path.

Revealing searchlight of the truth,
With softening rays to make us ruth.

Like Christ, who set it in motion,
Serving still with great devotion.

No wonder that its sunrise hues
Exhaust the spectrum of delight.

SONRISE

The promised Christ Child comes,
Witness of Truth, Champion of Right.

Missionary to the entire globe,
Creator and Savior of us all.

Climber of cruel Mount Calvary,
Revealer of the heart's intent.

Friend of every man and woman,
Calmer of the winds and waves.

God for all eternity,
Renewer of the penitent.

Giver of all life and health,
Source of soul's & body's wealth.

Forgiver of our sinful past,
Reviver of our sleepy souls.

Intercessor for us all,
Sonrise of God's plan to save us.

Healer of all wounds,
Lead us on our way to Heaven.

The Way, the Truth, the Light,
Lord of mercy, grace amazing.

Creator of all and our salvation,
Preserving all things in creation.

Lord of Glory, Son, and Spirit,
All our praise You surely merit.

A Palm Sunday Psalm

How low Christ bends;
   how high He rises.

Time and space cannot contain Him;
   yet the prison pit of hell He knew.

So pure His heart;
   so black His guilt.

So deep His grief;
   so full His joy.

So dark His death;
   so bright His rising.

So bitter His defeat;
   so utter His victory.

So humble His condescension;
   so exalted His ascension.

Such excess of extremes;
   that have set me free.

My heart is full of wonder;
   this my soul does well to ponder.

Amen
   and Amen.

INJ · OEB

BEHOLD, THE GOAT OF GOD

Doesn't that title sound wrong? John the Baptist said, "Look, the Lamb of God, who takes away the sins of the world" (Jn. 1:29). So, why am a calling Him the goat of God?

Once during a trip to Frankenmuth, Michigan, we stopped at Brunner's Christmas store and enjoyed looking at Christmas decorations from many lands. There we found a goat made out of straw. "What is that doing here?" I wondered aloud. My wife Ruth-Esther informed me that straw goats are a traditional Christmas symbol in Finland. Why?

We prefer to picture Christ as a lamb, a cute, fluffy lamb. This is certainly biblical. "We all, like sheep, have gone astray, each of us has turned to his own way; and the Lord has laid on Him the iniquity of us all" (Is. 53:6). Because Jesus is the sacrificial lamb, we decorate our churches with lambs. Our home decorations for Christmas and Holy Week may include a lamb or two. But why would anyone want a mangy goat in their church or home? The answer is in Leviticus 16:7-10:

> Then he [Aaron] is to take the two goats and present them before the Lord at the entrance to the Tent of Meeting. He is to casts lots for the two goats—one lot for the Lord and the other for the scapegoat. Aaron shall bring the goat whose lot falls to the Lord and sacrifice it for a sin offering. But the goat chosen by lot as the scapegoat shall be presented alive before the Lord to be used for atonement by sending it into the desert as a scapegoat.

A scapegoat bears the blame for others. On Yom Kippur, the Day of Atonement, the scapegoat bore the blame for the people of God as it was sent out into the desert to be torn apart by wild animals.

Jesus is the scapegoat who bears the blame of all humanity. On Good Friday, the fulfillment of Yom Kippur, He bore the blame for all our rebelliousness. Golgotha was a place of execution, a desert of death. There, like the predators of the wilderness, His enemies tore at Him with thorns, nails, and barbed criticism. His Heavenly Father drove Him out to this wilderness to perish, so that we might never endure eternal death in hell.

Although a scruffy old goat is not a pretty sight, it is an apt, biblical description of Christ. He is the scapegoat of the whole world. It doesn't sound very complimentary, but it wonderfully describes the crowning achievement of His mission to earth.

Behold Jesus, the goat of God.

What Jesus Dreaded Most

There it was again! Jesus had seen it before. How it repulsed Him, but look He must. There it was still—all our evil dreams in one hideous nightmare.

Even from His childhood it was with Him—the terrible vision of what was to come. His mother sensed it, feeling the cruel point of the sword which would pierce through her own soul also.

His friends sensed it too. Why was He sometimes so quiet and full of heaviness? What did He mean, "The time will come"? What did He mean, "First, the Son of Man must suffer many things"?

Now as they gathered in the Garden of Gethsemane following the Passover meal, He warned, "Watch and pray. My soul is exceedingly sorrowful even unto death." He had always known—and now it was nearly upon Him! Tomorrow the dreaded event would happen. A vast and fearful shudder surged like a tidal wave over the seawall of His soul, as if to smother His spirit.

So He knelt and pleaded, "If it is at all possible, take this cup away. Its unmentionable, gagging corruption shocks every sense I possess. Must it be, Father? This devil's cocktail, composite of all evil—must I drink it? Must I be made guilty of every person's sin to clear their record? Is there no other way? Yet, if I must, I will. Yes, if You, Father, say this terror is the only way to gain their liberation, then not My will, but Yours, be done."

The prayer was of a man afraid, a man in agony. No wonder "his sweat was like drops of blood falling to the ground" (Lk. 22:44). Still, he would never need to feel ashamed of this fear. For, although He was holy, a massive truck load of all the wretched garbage of human evil would soon be dumped on Him, and He would suffocate under it. No wonder He dreaded its approach.

Yet, with courage beyond our imagination, Jesus boldly faced what was coming: utter humiliation, terrifying isolation from God, crushing guilt and shame, as He battled sin, hell, and Satan—and won!

Have you ever received what Jesus Christ won for you? If not, repent of your sins and receive His precious pardon today. If you have it already, cherish it more dearly than ever.

> *Dear Savior, Your love purchased us at such a great price. Help us to glorify You, no matter what fears assail us. Amen.*

Always the Same

Who is yesterday,
today—always?
Jesus!

Who is Alpha
and Omega?
Jesus!

Whom never old,
prophets foretold?
Jesus!

Whose agony　　　Whose conviction　　　Ever steady
Gethsemane?　　　brought crucifixion?　　mercy ready?
Jesus'!　　　　　　Jesus'!　　　　　　　　Jesus!

Who braved the grave
the lost to save?
Jesus!

Who kept His word,
broke death's sharp sword?
Jesus!

Sent the Spirit
so we'd hear it?
Jesus!

Who rose to rule,
earth His footstool?
Jesus!

Ascended high,
His coming nigh?
Jesus!

Still enters hearts
new life to start?
Jesus!

So believe in
and rely on
Jesus!

The white and gold lily of Easter Morning has its roots deep down in the black mud and darkness of Good Friday.

EASTER—A NEW DAWN

Christ comes into our souls
   like a new dawn,
      a new day, a new hope,
         a new life that will last forever.

The resurrection of the Son of God
   is intentional.
      For many years before
         He told it would come to be.

The resurrection of the Crucified
   has legal force.
      It signs our pardon papers
         with the approving signature of Heaven.

The empty tomb of Jesus Christ
   is practical.
      My empty life, by sin laid waste
         Is now full, yes, meaningful.

The conquest of death and hell
   is perpetual.
      Not fleeting reprieve,
         but everlasting release.

The risen Savior of the World
   is personal.
      My life, my death are in His hands.
         Because He lives, I live.

The promise of life eternal
   is yours to have.
      Hurry to sign up today
         by repentance and faith in Christ.

Then Jesus will rise in your soul
   like a new dawn,
      a new day, a new hope,
         a new life that will last forever.

Lord Jesus, let Your Easter dawn in me!

MIRACLES! MIRACLES! MIRACLES!

The great events of Christ's crucifixion and resurrection so dominate the scene of Holy Week that many other miracles go unheralded. Marvel at all He accomplished in those days.

- The resurrection of Lazarus (Jn. 11:43-44)
- The miracle of the Lord's Supper (Lk. 22:8-38)
- The healing of Malchus' ear (Luke 22: 50-51)
- Angels strengthen Christ in the Garden (Lk. 22:43)
- His captors all fall on their backs (Jn. 18:4-6)
- The prophetic dream of Pilate's wife (Mt. 27:19)
- Jesus' prayer, "Father forgive them" (Lk. 23:34)
- The darkness at noonday (Mt. 27:45)
- The last-minute conversion of the thief (Lk. 23:39-43)
- The Centurion convinced of Jesus' divinity (Mk. 15:39)
- The earthquake as He died (Mt. 27:51)
- Many graves opened and the dead raised (Mt. 27:52)
- The veil of the Temple torn from top to bottom (Mk. 15:38)
- The guards at the grave prove ineffective (Mt. 27:66-28:4)

JESUS DOES THE LAUNDRY

Doing the laundry—what a menial task. Filthy clothes, sweaty underwear, grass-stained jeans, muddy socks all challenge our efforts to clean them.

I recall the toil of wash day for my mother, who washed for a family of ten without today's efficient washing machines, modern detergents, and wrinkle-free clothes. I can see her hauling water to three large tubs: one for soaking and scrubbing, one for rinsing, and one for bleaching. To squeeze out the water, she cranked the clothes through rollers. Every item of wet clothing she shook out and hung on the line to dry in the hot sun. Later she would press out the wrinkles with a heavy iron. Amazingly, every Monday she performed these daunting tasks with a cheerful spirit. How did she manage it? With maternal love she anticipated the finished product, visualizing her eight children seated in church on Sunday dressed in white shirts and trousers.

Not only clothes get dirty and stained, but souls as well, spattered with sins that reek and offend the holy God, keeping Him at a distance though He longs to be close. The Lord loves to see His children in clean clothing of the soul, their behavior inoffensive to His eyes. So why doesn't He tell us to get busy and scrub our moral clothes till they are clean and pure? Because we can't. David, recognizing his inability to clean his own dirty laundry, pleaded repentantly, "Create in me a pure heart, O God" (Ps. 51:10).

Would the Almighty God stoop to such a menial task? My mother's cheerful attitude on wash day is exactly the spirit the Bible tells us our Savior displayed as He undertook our redemption and renewal by the blood of the cross. He anticipated the final product: "For the joy set before him [He] endured the cross, scorning its shame" (Heb. 12:2). "Christ loved the church and gave Himself up for her to make her holy, cleansing her by the washing with water through the word, and to present her to himself as a radiant church, without stain or wrinkle or any other blemish, but holy and blameless" (Eph. 5:25-27).

Just as Mom visualized us all sitting in church dressed in white, so God gives us a vision. John reports,

> There before me was a great multitude that no one could count, from every nation, tribe, people and language, standing before the throne and in front of the Lamb. They were wearing white robes.... They have washed their robes and made them white in the blood of the Lamb (Rev. 7:9, 14).

Jesus does the laundry, not only for you and me, but for everyone in all the world. He was not too proud to volunteer for such a menial task. What a Savior!

POETRY DEFINED

Coleridge said:
 "Poetry is
  the best words
   in the best order."

Let me say:
 "Christian poetry is
  the best words
   in the best order
    about the Best One."

Jesus Is the Key

Romans 7 & 8   Revelation 1:18

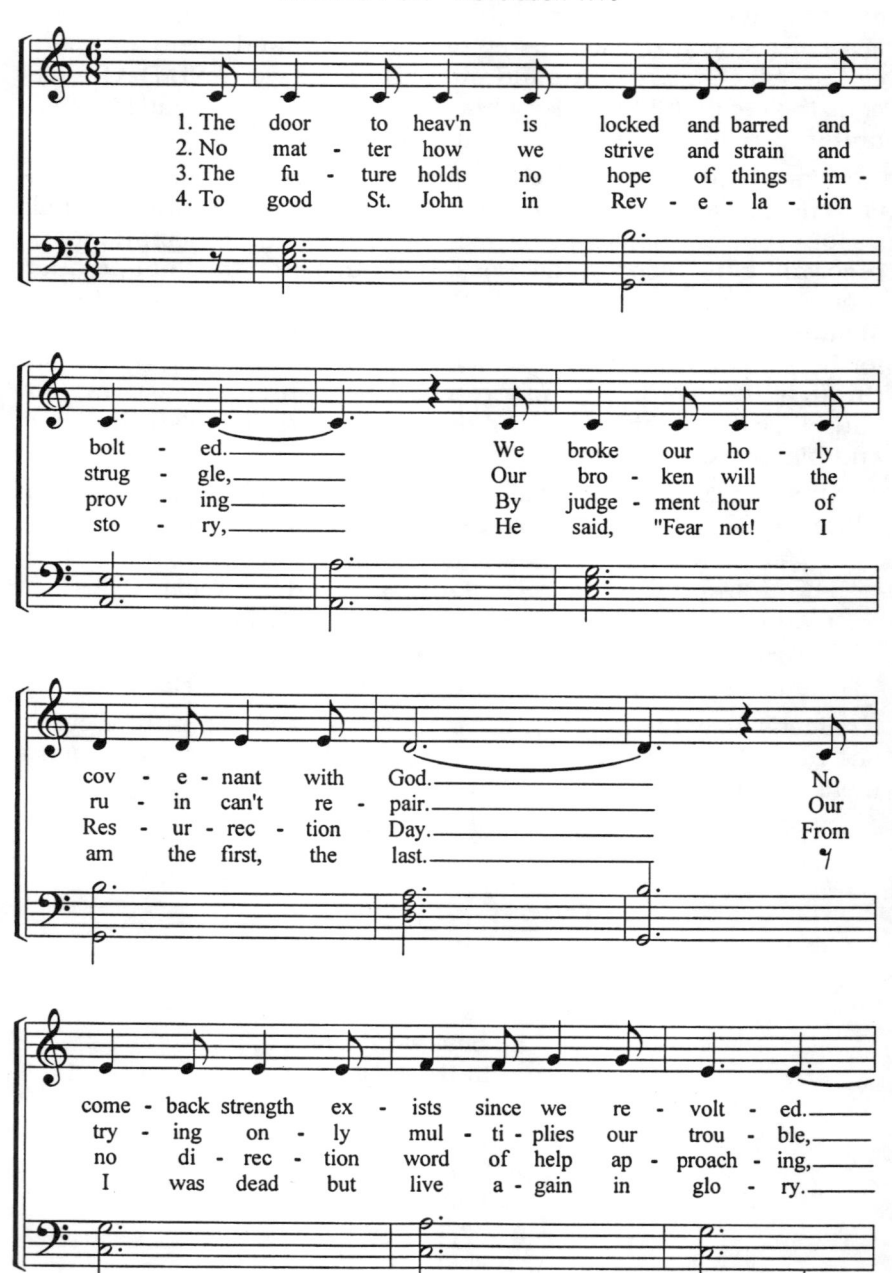

1. The door to heav'n is locked and barred and bolted. We broke our holy covenant with God. No come-back strength exists since we revolted.
2. No matter how we strive and strain and struggle, Our broken will the ruin can't repair. Our trying only multiplies our trouble.
3. The future holds no hope of things improving. By judgement hour of Resurrection Day. From no direction word of help approaching,
4. To good St. John in Revelation story, He said, "Fear not! I am the first, the last. I was dead but live again in glory."

CHRIST'S INFLUENCE   37

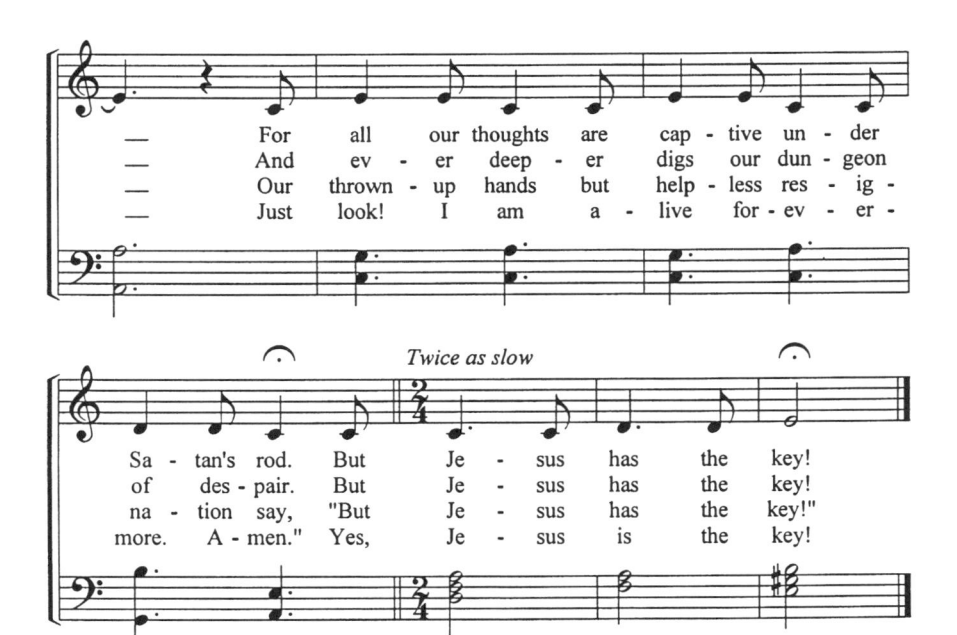

(Lyrics under music:)

	For	all	our	thoughts	are	cap -	tive	un - der
	And	ev - er	deep - er			digs	our	dun - geon
	Our	thrown - up	hands	but		help -	less	res - ig -
	Just	look!	I	am	a -	live	for -	ev - er -

Twice as slow

Sa - tan's rod.	But	Je - sus	has	the	key!
of des - pair.	But	Je - sus	has	the	key!
na - tion say,	"But	Je - sus	has	the	key!"
more. A - men."	Yes,	Je - sus	is	the	key!

5. What does this mean for us? Let's listen to Him.
   "I have the keys of hell and death, as well."
   So, therefore, now there is no condemnation.
   For those who trust in Christ are free and safe from hell.
   Look! Jesus is the key!

6. Let's, trusting, use the key of our great God's Son.
   Walk in the Spirit. Leave old ways behind.
   Deny the flesh, and claiming full adoption,
   Be more than conquer'rs now through Him whose love is true.
   Yes, He has set us free!

Words and melody by Ottomar E. Bickel
Harmonization by Ruth–Esther Hillila–Bickel

Who Is the Rock?

"You are my Father, my God, the Rock my Savior." Psalm 89:26

NOTE: Read this poem from the bottom line upward.

"He is the rock of my salvation."
I step into my Father's home.
Heaven's high doorstep stone,
Therefore, upon Christ,

Otherwise unscalable.
Stepping stone to salvation,
The only means of elevation,
Now, the very opposite;
A rock that would have crushed me,
Who, is that rock, but Jesus Christ?

And fear and tempest fill the night.
When the whole world is shaking
That will never, ever move
A rock to stand on squarely

New Verse for "His Name Is Wonderful"

How truly good He is.
Full thanks and honor give,
Trusting His Name alone,
Jesus, my Lord.
He is the Prince of Life,
Yet bore for me the strife,
His name is Wonderful,
Jesus, my Lord.
He's the true God's Son,
The light of all wisdom,
Yet sacrificed for me.
My life's now His alone,
Safe in the midst of storm,
His home as mine I own,
Jesus, my Lord.

3

How to Be Saved

Guard against the Interceptor

Think of Satan as a football defensive back who tries to deflect or intercept the pass intended for the pass receiver. Here are examples of some of his tactics.

1. False assumptions. A teenager smiled as he told his pastor about coming to Christ last weekend through the preaching of a visiting evangelist. "How is it," his pastor asked him, "that you did not hear the gospel when I preached it to you these many years?" The young man reflected a moment, "As a little kid, when I heard you talking so loudly from the pulpit, I assumed God was scolding me."

Satan had deceived him into hearing the loving call of God as accusations.

2. Fat ears. In a Bible class, a lady in her fifties shared, "For years I considered myself a good Christian. I was raised in the church, baptized, confirmed, attended every Sunday, and worked hard on committees. But I seldom read the Bible and didn't listen to sermons. 'I've heard all that before,' I told myself. Then one Sunday, I opened my big fat ears and started listening. It dawned on me that I really was a sinner who someday would die and be judged by God. For the first time I saw my only hope of surviving was Jesus. Now I am trusting in Him alone, thirsting for God, and hungering for the Word."

Since Satan had provided church activity as a substitute security, she had never really listened. Finally, the Holy Spirit gave her "ears to hear" what everyone needs to hear.

3. Not that bad. A young woman who had grown up in the church, when asked what she was depending on to get to heaven, answered immediately that she was trusting in Jesus Christ alone. Then she added, "and I've never done anything really wrong."

Such mixing of faith in Christ with trust in one's self is yet another trick of Satan. Self-idolatry will save no one.

4. Feathers. A white-haired man gave this testimony. "As a child, I won pins for Sunday school attendance and prizes for memorizing Bible verses. These were feathers in my cap. In the youth group I was elected president. Another feather in my cap. Later, they made me head usher, then an elder, then chairman of the elders. More and more feathers. Finally, I was president of the congregation. I had so many feathers, I thought I could fly to heaven! Thank God, He led someone to ask me what I was counting on to get to heaven. When I told her about my feathers, she tactfully informed me that all my feathers would burn up in judgment. And then she showed me Jesus."

Many have died counting on feathers rather than Christ.

Luther warned that if a person only knows about Jesus intellectually, but never claims Him as Savior, he or she will miss heaven by eighteen inches—the distance from the head to the heart.

In football a completed pass is not merely close. It is caught.

New Verse for "You'll Never Walk Alone"

    For the Lord of the storm
      who spoke calm to the sea,
        can speak perfect peace to your heart.
    For He conquered death's power
      for you and for me
        when He hung on the cross in the dark.
    He who rose from the dead,
      cleared the pathway ahead,
      will now guide and lead you home.
    Trust Him, trust Him!
      With Christ in your soul
      know you'll never walk alone,
      you'll never walk alone.

Whom Does God Choose?

The Apostle Paul said God chose:
- not many wise after the flesh
- not many mighty
- not many noble
- the foolish things of the world
- weak things
- lowly, despised things
- even the things that are not

Yes, God doesn't select only big shots, but also:
- the nobodies
- the lowly zeros
- those considered ignorant and inferior
- the common people
- the plain
- the ordinary
- the average
- the simple
- the poor
- those ashamed of their sinful frailties

How about you? Are you:
- too popular to be part of the Christian minority?
- too educated to learn the Bible's way of salvation?
- too sophisticated to engage in "foolish" witnessing?
- too prominent to declare your friendship with Christ?
- too influential to let Christ's influence on you show?
- too rich to need the treasure found in a field?
- too bejeweled to desire the pearl of great price?
- too attractive to desire the beauty of the Lord?
- too strong and virile to need the Helper of the weak?
- too secure to need the Rock of Ages?
- too self-sufficient to need the Supplier of our need?
- too high and mighty to bow before the King of kings?
- too distinguished to honor the Lord of lords?
- too pure to need the cleansing of His blood?
- too successful to lean on Him who said: "It is finished!"?
- too proud to humble yourself so He might lift you up?

FISHING FOR SOULS

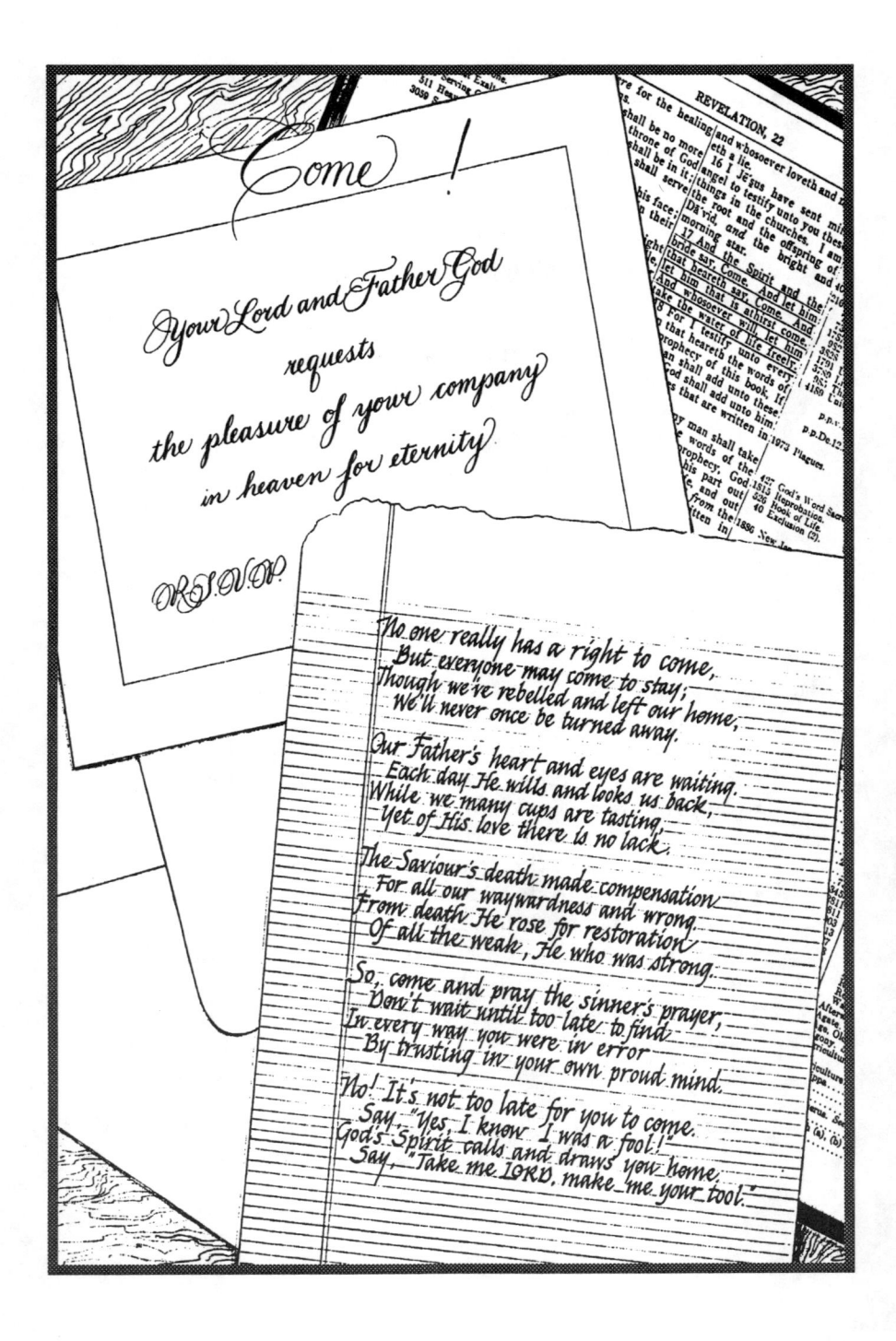

Come!

*Your Lord and Father God
requests
the pleasure of your company
in heaven for eternity.*

R.S.V.P.

No one really has a right to come,
　But everyone may come to stay;
Though we've rebelled and left our home,
　We'll never once be turned away.

Our Father's heart and eyes are waiting,
　Each day He wills and looks us back;
While we many cups are tasting,
　Yet of His love there is no lack.

The Saviour's death made compensation
　For all our waywardness and wrong,
From death He rose for restoration
　Of all the weak, He who was strong.

So, come and pray the sinner's prayer;
　Don't wait until too late to find
In every way you were in error
　By trusting in your own proud mind.

No! It's not too late for you to come.
　Say, "Yes, I know I was a fool!"
God's Spirit calls and draws you home,
　Say, "Take me LORD, make me your tool."

Blood Cleanser

Some people are disturbed when they hear Christians speak about being "cleansed by the blood of the Lamb." But when the Bible explains this idea, it makes surprising sense.

St. John says, "The blood of Jesus, his Son, purifies us from all sin" (1 Jn. 1:7). Usually we think of blood as a messy substance which requires a lot of effort to clean up. Even so, John calls the blood of Christ a purifier, a cleanser, a spot remover. How can this be?

Most of us live oblivious to the fact that just on the other side of our skin six quarts of blood course through 60,000 miles of blood vessels. We take this "fluid organ" for granted, until we lose some of it. When I was seven years old, a .22 caliber bullet was shot through my hand. I didn't cry until I saw blood gush out. Then I was certain I was going die.

What is the purpose of blood? Like mail carriers, blood cells deliver oxygen and food to every cell in your body. After dropping off their care package, your blood cells then go to work as garbage collectors. They gather carbon dioxide and send it to the lungs for you to exhale. They collect urea and deliver it to the kidneys for elimination. If your blood cells went on strike, your whole body would soon become bloated with carbon dioxide and urea, a predicament more serious than growing mountains of trash in a city during a garbage collectors' strike.

Now the Bible phrase "washed in the blood" doesn't sound so strange. What better illustration could God use for the cleansing which Christ grants us through His blood?

His death confronted all evil where it was and brought it under the cleansing corpuscles of divine holiness. His blood daily carries away the impurities of our sin. The Old and New Testament writers agree, "without the shedding of blood there is no forgiveness" (Heb. 9:22). The multitudes gathered before God's throne are there enjoying His presence only because they "have washed their robes and made them white in the blood of the Lamb" (Rev. 7:14).

By means of the blood of Jesus, anyone can confidently enter heaven free of sin. So, receive Him by repentance and faith, and His cleansing is yours. What He begins, He will keep doing for you as steadily as a heartbeat.

The Names of Your Peace

Yes, you can be sure of heaven.
Hear the names of Jesus Christ.
As the Rock of Our Salvation,
He guarantees eternal life.

Your Cornerstone, your Righteousness,
Morning Star yet Sunrise too,
Your Master cloaked in Servant's dress,
Messenger of Love to you.

Wonderful, Counselor, God of Might,
Everlasting Father,
Prince of Peace and God of Light,
Word that was Creator.

The Son of God whom angels bless,
Immanuel, God with Us here;
The Son of Man whom angels bless,
As holy manger-child appears.

The Sin-Bearer, your load He bore,
Uplifted Savior against the sky;
Advocate and Intercessor,
For thieves He opened paradise.

Seeker of the Lost, He finds you,
As Good Shepherd leads you,
To Living Water guides you,
As Bread of Life feeds you,
As Great Physician heals you,
As Divine Teacher trains you,
As True Vine sustains you,
As Prince of Life raises you,
As Judge of All praises you,
As Lord of Heaven welcomes you.

Thank You, Lord Jesus Christ,
Lamb that was Slain,
Pearl of Great Price.
Thank You, for living up to Your names!

How to Be Saved   45

WHAT CAN MATCH CHRIST'S RESURRECTION?

DEATH IS SWALLOWED UP IN VICTORY. 1 COR. 15:54

What can match Christ's res-ur-rec-tion? Al - - le - lu - ia!
Since my LORD a - rose in glo-ry, Al - - le - lu - ia!
Ev - er in my LORD a-bid-ing, Al - - le - lu - ia!

O - ver-com-ing cru - ci - fix - ion Al - - le - lu - ia!
I will ev - er tell the sto-ry, Al - - le - lu - ia!
And by prayer in Him con-fid-ing, Al - - le - lu - ia!

Full for-give-ness, His to give. Al - - le - lu - ia!
How He pays my debt of sins Al - - le - lu - ia!
May I nest the Ho-ly Dove, Al - - le - lu - ia!

Since He lives, I, too shall live. Al - - le - lu - ia!
And for me full vic-t'ry wins. Al - - le - lu - ia!
Die to self and learn His love. Al - - le - lu - ia! A-men.

WORDS: Ottomar E. Bickel, 1985
MUSIC: Arr. from *Lyra Davidica*, 1708

EASTER HYMN
7.7.7.7, Alleluias

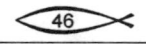

LIFE BILLBOARDS

Suppose you were driving along the highway and saw a billboard announcing: "I can give you life. Call 333-7777." How might you respond to this offer?

1. Maybe you would chuckle, "They've got to be kidding."
2. You might be perturbed, "What kind of scam is this?"
3. Perhaps you would express doubt, "If a business can really provide life, they aren't going to hand it out for free."
4. Or you might be angered, "Who are they to claim they can give life?"
5. Upon reflection, you might think, "Wouldn't it be wonderful if this offer were true? Maybe I should call the number and check it out."

Yes, a billboard claiming, "I can give you life" would cause quite a stir.

Do you know what? If you read the Gospel of John, you will find something like that billboard. In chapter after chapter, Jesus announces He has something to bestow—LIFE!

Here is a list of Jesus' amazing statements. Consider them one by one. How will you respond to His offer?

> Jesus told Nicodemus, "For God so loved the world that he gave his one and only Son, that whoever believes in him shall not perish but have eternal life.... Whoever believes in the Son has eternal life, but whoever rejects the Son will not see life, for God's wrath remains on him" (3:16, 36).

> Jesus told the woman at the well, "Whoever drinks the water I give him will never thirst. Indeed, the water I give him will become in him a spring of water welling up to eternal life" (4:14).

> To some Jews who disagreed with Him, Jesus argued, "I tell you the truth, whoever hears my word and believes him who sent me has eternal life and will not be condemned; he has crossed over from death to life" (5:24).

> To the crowds who had been fed by the multiplication of the loaves and fishes, Jesus declared, "I am the bread of life. He who comes to me will never go hungry, and he who believes in me will never be thirsty.... For my Father's will is that everyone who looks to the Son and believes in him

shall have eternal life, and I will raise him up at the last day" (6:35, 40).

To the crowds gathered on a feast day, Jesus shouted, "Whoever believes in me, as the Scripture has said, streams of living water will flow from within him" (7:38).

Again, he told the people, "I am the light of the world. Whoever follows me will never walk in darkness, but will have the light of life" (8:12).

Using sheep-shepherd imagery, Jesus taught, "I am the gate for the sheep.... whoever enters through me will be saved. He will come in and go out, and find pasture. The thief comes only to steal and kill and destroy; I have come that they may have life, and have it to the full. I am the good shepherd. The good shepherd lays down his life for the sheep" (10:7, 8, 10, 11).

To Martha, whose brother Lazarus had died and would soon be raised from the grave, Jesus explained, "I am the resurrection and the life. He who believes in me will live, even though he dies" (11:25).

He comforted His disciples with this promise, "In my Father's house are many rooms; if it were not so, I would have told you. I am going there to prepare a place for you. And if I go and prepare a place for you, I will come back and take you to be with me that you also may be where I am.... I am the way and the truth and the life. No one comes to the Father except through me" (14:2-3, 6).

The night before He died for the sins of all people, He prayed, "Father, the time has come. Glorify your Son, that your Son may glorify you. For you granted him authority over all people that he might give eternal life to all those you have given him. Now this is eternal life: that they may know you, the only true God, and Jesus Christ, whom you have sent" (17:1-3).

So how will you respond to Jesus offer? Will you laugh it off as a joke? Will you avoid it like a scam? Will you question whether the gift of eternal life is free, no strings attached? Will you doubt Jesus has the power to give you life? Or will you believe and receive what He offers?

Humbly confess your sin and weakness to Jesus, and by faith receive the gift He offers freely—Eternal Life.

48 FISHING FOR SOULS

He is our Life

1. He is our life, His life the light of men.
2. Who else dare say, 'I am of life the Light'?
3. Come to the Spring where liv-ing wa-ters flow.

Christ Je-sus fills us full of hope a-gain.
Who else dis-pels the gloom of our dark night?
Je-sus in-vites us; quick-ly let us go,

Be-cause He lives, we too shall live. A-men.
His light is true, re-pla-ces wrong with right.
There quench our thirst, the deep thirst of the soul.

Al - le - lu - ia! Al - le - lu - ia!
Al - le - lu - ia! Al - le - lu - ia!
Al - le - lu - ia! Al - le - lu - ia! A-men.

WORDS: Ottomar E. Bickel, Based on the great 'I ams' of Jesus
MUSIC: R. Vaughan Williams, 1906, arr.

SINE NOMINE
10, 10, 10 with Allelui

4 As Living Bread, He gives us all to eat,
His very self our nourishment and meat;
Our life and health eternal and complete.
Alleluia! Alleluia!

5 LORD of our lives and Shepherd of our souls,
He gave His life that we might all be whole;
A pastor true, He leads us to the fold.
Alleluia! Alleluia!

6 "I am the Life, the Truth, the only Way,
Just follow Me, trust in Me and obey,
To reach the Father and come home to stay."
Alleluia! Alleluia!

7 Christ boldly claimed, "I will the third day rise."
"I am the Resurrection and the Life,"
All who believe will conquer in death's strife.
Alleluia! Alleluia!

8 They who believe and trust Christ's sacrifice,
Shall live forever, cross and death suffice;
No longer living for themselves but Christ.
Alleluia! Alleluia!

9 Christ went before, prepares in heaven a place.
Those who precede us and have won the race,
Now urge us onward till we see His face.
Alleluia! Alleluia!

Alleluia!

WHAT GRADE WOULD YOU GIVE JESUS?

When I preached in Kaiserslautern, West Germany in 1988, several people spoke to me and said my sermon was "dull." I thanked them for the compliment. You see, in German, the word *toll* is pronounced "dull," but it means "the best." Thus, their evaluation, which sounded like blunt criticism in English, was actually the highest compliment in German.

If you were called upon to evaluate Jesus Christ, what grade would you give Him? In Mark 7:37, His disciples said, "He does all things well." He made the deaf hear and the mute speak. He made the lepers clean and the prostitutes pure in the eyes of God. No wonder the disciples gave Him an A+. Their evaluation was correct in every language. Christ deserves our praise, because He earned it with deeds of power, compassion, and pardon.

We like to excel, and we fish for compliments. When we can't do something remarkable ourselves, we identify with others who are successful. We become fans who brag and exaggerate. We give star performers impressive nicknames. The best basketball player on earth is called Air Jordan because he seems to fly through the air to make spectacular shots. How we exaggerate the achievements of our heroes—Awesome! Fabulous! Number One!

However, in the case of Jesus Christ, it is impossible to exaggerate. He is unmatched by anyone. All His fine attributes and achievements are totally true. He often prefaced His remarks with, "Verily, verily," which means, "What I'm now going to tell you is true truth." He didn't just speak the truth. He lived it. "For in Christ all the fullness of the Deity lives in bodily form, and you have been given fullness in Christ..." (Col. 2:9-10).

On the cross Jesus graded His own paper and gave Himself an A+ when He declared, "It is finished" (Jn. 19:30). "By one sacrifice he has made perfect forever those who are being made holy" (Heb. 10:14). And so we may be bold to enter the Most Holy Place by the blood of Jesus.

Try as we may, we can never exaggerate anything good about Jesus. No one who trusts in Him can ever trust in Him too much. So why not trust in Him now, and forever?

4
LIFE IN THE SPIRIT

CHRISTMAS MYSTERY

Let's do a word-association test. Who do you think of when I say "Christmas"?

Who comes to your mind? Perhaps the Christ Child, Mary, Joseph, the shepherds, the angels, the innkeeper, the Heavenly Father, King Herod, the wise men, or the martyred children of Bethlehem.

Amid all these characters, we tend to overlook one key actor—the Holy Spirit. Is it because He's not involved? Hardly! Regarding Christ's birth the Apostles' Creed mentions only two persons: "Conceived of the Holy Spirit, born of the Virgin Mary." And He's mentioned first. So how come we didn't mention Him first?

Following the nativity, Simeon went to the temple and identified the Christ Child, because "the Holy Spirit was upon him" and "it had been revealed to him by the Holy Spirit" (Lk. 2:25, 26).

Without the Holy Spirit, Christ would not have been born. So why don't we think of him in connection with Christmas?

St. Paul said that the Holy Spirit's work is to glorify Christ, not Himself. He purposely stands in the wings and leaves the stage spotlight for Jesus. Jesus glorifies the Father, and the Father glorifies the Son and Holy Spirit. In the Holy Trinity, each applauds and draws attention to the other. That's God's style.

So let's copy God's style, The Holy Spirit shows us the way. Keep the spotlight on Christ, not on yourself. Glory be to Jesus!

THE FIRST SHALL BE LAST

> When I come first,
> I'm at my worst.
> When I come last,
> I'm at my best.
> So Jesus, You be first.

CONTINUAL BAPTISM

"Our Lord and Master, Jesus Christ, in saying; 'Repent ye,' etc., intended that the whole life of believers should be penitence." First Thesis of Luther's 95 Theses.

> My way of life needs to be clean.
> Give, Lord, great love of holiness.
> Let every stain in me be seen,
> that I may all my faults confess,
> the washing of my Baptism claim
> each day afresh, cleansed by Your name.
> Now live a new life constantly
> in faith and love and purity.
>
> As I confess the deeds and words
> that grieved you in temptation's hour,
> baptize me now again, dear Lord,
> You, who baptize with Spirit's power.
> I claim a cleansing by Your blood,
> anoint my soul with Your pure love;
> pour in upon me like a flood
> Your gifts and graces from above.
>
> Thus, each day is a new beginning,
> Sins erased and heart swept clean
> The Jesus way.
> Mercy, new to me each morning,
> Restored by Christ, refreshed, redeemed.
> It's Jesus' day.

Finders, Keepers!

If you knew
    exactly where
    to dig in the ground
    or dive in the ocean,

you could find
    a great wealth
    of buried gold and treasure
    and rich natural resources.

It's all there—waiting!

So with the Bible.
    True treasure
    will surely be found
    by those who seek it.

Just ask the Spirit
    to direct
    where you should dig
    and you will surely find it.

It's all there—waiting!

You'll find Jesus,
    golden treasure,
    pearl of great price
    for your very own.

He is there—waiting!

BIBLE MARKING SYSTEM

What would you do if you dropped a diamond ring into a hay stack? You would dig and search until you had recovered it. And if you were able to find it, you certainly wouldn't toss it back into the hay stack for safe keeping!

Yet, as we read the Bible, we often misplace God's glorious treasures. A Bible marking system will help you keep track of special passages in the Scripture's enormous hay stack of verses.

Color Key

RED	The Gospel - Redemption - Repentance Forgiveness - Conversion - Faith Promises of the Messiah and Fulfillment
PURPLE	Sacrifice - The Priesthood - The Temple Christ's Sacrifice and Suffering Persecution and Martyrdom of Believers Baptism - The Lord's Supper - Royalty
GREEN	Discipleship - Christian Life and Growth Prayer - Praise - Worship The Church - Call of God - Public Ministry Witness - Missions - Serving Others
BLUE	Resurrection - Immortality - Life - Heaven
YELLOW	Glory of God - Attributes of God Angels - Miracles God's Promises - Comfort
ORANGE	The Holy Spirit - Holy Scripture Prophets - God's Revealing of Himself
BROWN	Advice and Admonition to Believers Discipline of Believers
BLACK	The Law - Warning - Sin - Judgment Death - Hell - Sorrow and Sadness - Satan

Bible Column Symbols

☧	Messianic prophecy and fulfillment	✝	The Crucifixion
℘	Christian comfort	P	Prayer
⌒	The Holy Spirit	A	Angels
△	The Trinity	G	Attributes of God
♕	Jesus is God	♡	Love
♁	Baptism	🍞	Lord's Supper
📖	The Bible	📕	The Law
🌅	Morning	D	Discipleship
⊕	Missions	C	Children

Gifts are for Sharing

1. A Christian always shares. God gave us all we own.
   He shares because He cares; Sees all he owns a loan
   from Him, who first left all, to give His
   precious life that we might live.

2. It's now Christ's life we share, God's gifts are not our own.
   So, when we really care we won't serve self alone,
   but use our gifts shown in the Word to
   serve the Body of the LORD.

3. May we be much aware, in whom the Spirit lives,
   Of gifts and talents rare that God, the Spirit gives;
   that we may serve our fellow-man when
   he's in need, the best we can.

4. These good gifts from above let's seek from God with prayer,
   But most of all, His love, so that each gift we share
   displays the LORD's compassion for each
   hurting one, whose sins He bore. A - men.

WORDS: Ottomar E. Bickel, 1985
MUSIC: John Darwall, 1770

DARWALL'S 148th
6.6.6.6.8.8.

Second Wind for the Christian Walk

"My soul follows hard after thee, O God." Psalm 63:8, KJV

Daily brisk walking for a half-hour or so is perhaps the best method of keeping fit. By providing extra oxygen to the body, walking strengthens the heart, lungs, stomach, liver and circulatory system. Regular hiking can even build new blood vessels.

Walking with the Spirit is great spiritual exercise, as these texts from the King James Version indicate. As you read them, consider: How am I walking?

- "We... should walk in newness of life" (Rom. 6:4).
- "Walk not after the flesh, but after the Spirit" (Rom. 8:4).
- "Let us walk honestly" (Rom. 13:13)
- "Walk in the Spirit, and ye shall not fulfill the lust of the flesh" (Gal. 5:16).
- "For we are His workmanship, created in Christ Jesus unto good works, which God hath before ordained that we should walk in them" (Eph. 2:10).
- "Walk worthy of the vocation to which ye are called, with all lowliness and meekness, with long suffering, forbearing one another in love" (Eph. 4:1-2).
- "See, then, that ye walk circumspectly, not as fools but as wise" (Eph. 5:15).
- "That ye might walk worthy of the Lord unto all pleasing, being fruitful in every good work, and increasing in the knowledge of God" (Col. 1:10).
- "As ye have, therefore, received Christ Jesus the Lord, so walk ye in Him" (Col. 2:6).
- "Walk in wisdom toward them that are outside, redeeming the time" (Col. 4:5).
- "That ye would walk worthy of God, who hath called you unto His... glory" (1 Thes. 2:12).

In the book *Aerobics* Dr. Kenneth Cooper explains that if we exercise for only a brief period of time, it depletes the oxygen supply, and we tend to feel tired and may even experience chest pains. This is why many exercisers give up too soon. What a mistake! Continued walking causes us to breathe more deeply, which soon replaces the lost oxygen and even stockpiles an extra supply, enabling us to walk with ease for a long time. We call this pleasant result "getting our second wind."

Similarly, Christians who pray a little, read their Bible a little, obey a little, and witness a little are usually very tired and uncomfortable. What a mistake!

Better to follow hard after God, as David advised in Psalm 68. Pray hard, read much, obey much, witness repeatedly for days and weeks on end until the second wind time arrives when your soul no longer hurts but has grown marvelously strong and well.

Then you will agree with St. Paul: "I can do everything through him who gives me strength.... And my God will meet all your needs according to his glorious riches in Christ Jesus." (Phil. 4:13, 19).

So let's stretch our legs and continue in the Christian walk till we get our second wind, being filled with the Holy Spirit. He is our second wind. He is spiritual oxygen. When you are rich in the Spirit, you have second wind. You become airborne, lifted with wings as eagles.

Like a Drop of Water

Every word of God
is like a drop of water
in the sea
of Scripture,
teeming
with life and meaning
when you allow the
microscope of the Holy Spirit
to enlarge and
reveal it to you.

So also every Christian
is like a drop of water
in the great sea
of the church,
teeming
with life and potential
for God's use
when you allow
the indwelling Spirit
to reveal and empower
His plan.

Words In Tune

It was already late in my life
   when I was led
      to write in verse.
         Only twice or thrice before
           did I attempt
              to write in tune.

It seems very evident to me
   that poetry
      is symmetry
         of heart and soul and mind;
           a sensing of GOD
              in everything.

For when I stop to look and listen,
   I hear and see Him
      everywhere.
         He, from within, makes all things rhyme;
           for He's Himself
              in perfect tune.

So we are His art, His workmanship,
   created in CHRIST
      unto good works.
         His purpose is to fashion our lives
           into a poem
              of perfect praise.

How to Set a Church on Fire

My uncle tells the story
Of when he was a pastor
Long years ago in Kansas
Just at the thaw of spring.

As was their faithful habit
The flock had come together
From farms off in the distance
That sunny Sunday morn.

It was a large, old, frame church
That held the congregation,
Used for three generations,
Built when the West was young.

The service was in session,
Full force he was a-preachin',
That God the Holy Spirit
Might set their hearts on fire.

Then he became uneasy.
He sensed a restless stirring.
Next came a great commotion
As everyone smelled smoke!

He asked them to be quiet,
By rows to exit calmly.
The room was quickly empty,
All outside in the sun.

They looked up to the church roof
And saw there by the chimney,
A fire, from sparks ignited,
As large as any room.

No ladder and no water!
The people now were praying,
And everyone was wond'ring
How they might save their church.

One man looked 'round the church yard
And spied against the rail fence
A large left-over snowdrift,
Now melting in the sun.

He quickly formed a snowball.
With all his might he threw it.
All saw it arcing upward
And land amid the flames.

The fire kept right on burning!
But soon more than one hundred
Male members of the parish,
Attacked the fire with snow.

The air was full of snowballs!
At first the fire sputtered,
But when they all persisted,
It went completely out.

As they gave thanks together,
A sermon was not needed
To tell them how it happened
That their dear church was spared.

God worked for them a wonder
And taught them all a lesson:
When all will help together,
What can't be done, gets done.

When anywhere there's trouble,
In church-life or in home-life,
Let's gladly help together
In putting out the fire.

A church that so converges
On each one's need with prayer
Applies the 'snow' of Jesus,
Becomes a church 'on fire.'

Martin Luther Describes the Soul-Winner

Luther was altogether a soul-winner. He dueled for souls with Satan and won. He wielded the sword of the Spirit. His heart was in it, compelled by the love of Christ which he had received. Luther was taken up, in public and private, with one message: There is grace for sinners if they will repent and receive it by faith in Christ.

Below is my translation of Luther's eloquent description of a soul-winner. Honestly ask yourself: Does it describe me? If not, ask the Lord to give you so much joy in the gospel that the transformation will begin.

> When a Christian begins to know Christ as His Lord and Savior, through Whom he has been rescued from death, and has been brought under His lordship and inheritance, then his heart is permeated with God (*durchgottert*), so that he is driven to help others receive the same, because there is no greater joy for him than this treasure that he now knows Jesus.
>
> So he heads out in every direction, teaches and urges all others, boasts about the Gospel and witnesses of it to everyone, pleads and sighs that they might receive such grace.
>
> He has a restless spirit, while at the same time, possessing the greatest peace of mind himself in God's grace and forgiveness. Therefore, he cannot be motionless and relaxed, but instead contests for and strives with all his might, as one who lives for one purpose, that is, that he might spread more widely among people, God's honor and praise.
>
> From *Christliches Wegweiser* (1980), page 367.

5

SHARING GOOD NEWS

THE FIRST THING ON JESUS'S MIND

Nothing can happen in soul-winning until disciples go. Jesus could have dwelt on many other topics His last days on earth. However, the first and last thing on His mind was, "Go and make disciples of all nations" (Mt. 28:19).

On resurrection evening, Jesus told His disciples, "You are my witnesses!" (Lk. 24:48). He could hardly have gotten to the subject more quickly. It had to be first on His mind. In addition, He told them, "Peace be with you! As the Father has sent me, I am sending you" (Jn. 20:21). The Lord meant this not only for the Apostles, but for every Christian.

When He appeared to seven disciples at the Sea of Galilee, it was still His number one concern. "Feed My lambs. Feed My sheep" (Jn. 21:15, 17). When He ascended, it was all he talked about. "But you will receive power when the Holy Spirit comes on you; and you will be my witnesses in Jerusalem, and in all Judea and Samaria, and to the ends of the earth" (Acts 1:8).

Think of the whole scope of theology with all its topics and doctrines. Think of all the other subjects in the universe. Why did He emphasize this one? Accidental choice? Certainly not! He tells us to go, because He loves the lost.

As we observe the Christian Church today, is personal witness the first thing on its mind? Is it the first thing on your mind?

The risen Christ had just broken the chains of sin, death, and the devil—for all people of all time. The next thing on His mind? "Go! Go and tell! Show and tell! Yes, go! Go with God!"

Every Soul is Precious

PSALM 126

1. Ev'ry soul of man is precious, bought with Christ's blood as the price. God's great heart longs to restore us, by the Lamb's great sacrifice, to His household, where all saved souls Meet to praise and

2. But who's missing from the roll call, who's still left in the deep cold; Now and e-ver with-out hope in, with-out God in this lost world? Must I not with tears and plead-ing, call on them while

3. Lord for-give my fear-ful si-lence, give me nerve to speak up now. Ho-ly Spi-rit, fill my spir-it, give me right words teach me how to reach out with love and car-ing, weep-ing my Geth-

SHARING GOOD NEWS 65

(sheet music)

raise His name; where God, Father, Son and
there is time; Speak the Word that lights their
se - ma - ne, as did Je - sus, who then

Spir - it, us His own, for - e - ver claims.
dark - ness and guides them to heav'n sub - lime?
reached for each lost soul from Cal - va - ry.

WORDS: Ottomar E. Bickel
MUSIC: Thomas J. Williams, 1869-1944

EBENEZER
87 87 D

WITNESSING IN THE SPIRIT

"So the women hurried away from the tomb, afraid yet filled with joy, and ran to tell his disciples." Matthew 28:8

After years of war in foreign lands,
He returns home to the farm.
Hugs and kisses all around—
Except for Dad.
Youngest brother races out
Across the fields in youthful strides
To tell his father in breathless cries,
"Joe is home safe from the war!"
With news like that a boy can't walk.

So when speaking to others of Christ,
Sense the urgency and the joy.
You have news of breathless excitement
Truly worth running to tell.

A Short and Sweet Story

Let's keep it simple when we tell the lost the way to heaven.

1. Heaven is a free gift, not earned or deserved. "For the wages of sin is death, but the gift of God is eternal life in Christ Jesus, our Lord" (Rom. 6:32). We cannot earn heaven because we really are sinners. Face to face with the holy God, we would be rejected and condemned. God is so holy that "whoever keeps the whole law and yet stumbles at just one point is guilty of breaking all of it" (Jas. 2:10.) St. Paul says, "There is no difference, for all have sinned and fall short of the glory of God" (Rom. 3:23).

2. However, in His love, God found a means of escape which also satisfies His justice. The Father took His Son, who was true God, put Him in human form and then let Him be tempted in every way as we are tempted. There was one difference—Jesus did not sin. The next step of our salvation took place at the cross. There He placed the collective guilt of our sins on His Son. Long ago, the Prophet Isaiah had foretold, "The Lord has laid on him the iniquity of us all" (Isaiah 53:6). This means that in Christ we have already been to hell. Now there is a Savior for all people who can offer each of us a place in heaven paid for with His blood. "The blood of Jesus, his Son, purifies us from all sin" (1 Jn. 1:7).

3. Faith is more than just knowing about Christ or thinking highly of Him. God requires that we each repent of our sins and turn to Jesus. Therefore, faith is personally and consciously trusting in Jesus Christ alone for your salvation. Peter urged, "Repent and be baptized every one of you, in the name of Jesus Christ so that your sins may be forgiven" (Acts 2:38). Paul urged, "Believe on the Lord Jesus Christ, and you will be saved" (Acts 16:31). This is a standing offer for everyone. Faith takes hold of the saving hand of God. Then He leads us safely through the rest of our life, through our death and the judgment, and into heaven.

This is the short sweet story, as simple as 1, 2, 3. It has been written by a neighbor on an index card, spoken to a friend dying of cancer, told by a gas station attendant to a customer, and spoken to a neighbor at the kitchen table.

Though quickly expressed, when truly believed its impact lasts for eternity.

Dear Lord

A Soul-Winner's Prayer

What a joy to see
a soul won for thee
out of darkness and fears,
out of sin and from tears.

So make me to be,
obediently,
a witness for Jesus,
to tell how He frees us.

Give me Your Spirit,
so I can share it,
with Your words strong and clear,
overcoming all fear. Amen.

Caught by the Wrist

Please allow me to share with you my personal testimony.

Because I grew up in a parsonage, some may claim I was born with a spiritual silver spoon in my mouth. Yes, many advantages were mine. Our four grandparents were earnest Christians. Six of us boys entered the ministry. Our youngest brother died at age four confessing a child-like faith in Christ. But Christian faith must be personal. You don't inherit it. Preacher's kids can hit the skids too. Yet, if you are looking for a testimony of public disgrace and a dramatic rescue, you will be disappointed. God deserves all the credit. By His grace I trusted in Christ from my earliest recollections.

God has shown me His rescuing power several times. One winter day when I was in first grade, we all were running back into school after recess. Our path took us across a large iron grate in the center aisle. The bolts securing the grate had long ago disappeared. Down below in the basement stood the red hot furnace which heated our one-room school. When a hefty older boy running in front of me landed on the far edge of the grate, the edge near me flipped up, and I flew into the opening. Just as I was falling into the death trap below, an eighth-grade girl running behind me reached down, caught me by the wrist, and pulled me out as neatly as a circus acrobat. Her name was Luella. I've never forgotten. I could have died, but God had other plans for me. May He be praised!

Later at age eight, one night I lay in bed afraid during a violent thunderstorm, because lightening had struck our house once before. Amid the tempest I wondered, "If I died, how would God judge me?" I thought of my sins and confessed them. Then I reminded God, "Lord, You can't lie. Since I'm trusting in Jesus who died for my sins too, You will surely receive me." Someone caught me by the wrist. His name is Jesus. I haven't forgotten His name either.

Years later in my forties, one morning I crested a hill on a country road at the very moment that a big truck passed me in the oncoming lane. The eighteen-wheeler had appeared so suddenly that I thought, "What if it had been on my side?" As I drove on, three times I went through the motions of lurching into the ditch and then back onto the road. Five miles further down the road a car approached at high speed. When I saw one wheel cross the double lines, I didn't hesitate. I hit the ditch. As he passed me he was completely in my lane, but a split second had made the difference. I had never practiced escape tactics before, nor have I since. What did it mean? I concluded God let me experience His watchfulness and care in this special way to assure me that I belong to Him. "I have saved your soul, and I have visibly saved your life. So don't live for yourself, but for Him who died for you and rose again."

Special signs like this are not a necessity. God's Word is more than enough, but at times He chooses to add a personal touch. He does not lie. He is faithful. He can be trusted.

NORMAL CHRISTIAN LIFESTYLE

According to Acts 2, normal Christians:
- gather together
- are Spirit-filled
- witness the Gospel of Christ
- are repentant and gladly receive the Word
- receive Christ and are baptized
- are regular in Bible Study
- fellowship
- commune
- pray
- believe God performs miracles
- share their blessings and resources
- help the needy
- are in touch with other Christians, daily
- love God's house and go there often
- offer much hospitality
- meet in homes, in small groups
- express happiness and hope
- keep their eyes on Jesus
- praise God often
- have a good reputation
- are a pleasure to have around
- attract others
- multiply in number

These are the vital signs of normal Christianity. Have we settled for a watered down version which we now consider normal? It is not too late for God's Spirit to normalize us, to return us to what He accomplished in Acts 2.

I Must Speak

FOR WE CANNOT BUT SPEAK THE THINGS WHICH WE HAVE HEARD AND SEEN. ACTS 4:20

1. I must speak up for Jesus, I must confess my faith;
   I must tell how He saved us, I must proclaim His grace.
   Did He not die for all men? Did He not bear our shame?
   The gates of heaven open For those who name His Name.

2. The promise He has spoken Is true, forever sure.
   His word is still unbroken, His followers secure.
   May I stand by Him ever, As He has stood by me.
   May I deny Him never, Be proud His friend to be.

3. For this I need His Spirit, To make my will like steel.
   The test? I need not fear it. His helping hand is real.
   So, Lord, grant me the daring Your messenger to be,
   For ev'ry lost soul caring, As You have cared for me. A-men

WORDS: Ottomar E. Bickel 1990
MUSIC: Samuel S. Wesley, 1864

AURELIA
7,6,7,6 D.

EVANGELICAL IS OUR MIDDLE NAME

I am the pastor of a church called Zion Evangelical Lutheran. What a strange middle name. Many other churches also include "evangelical" in their name. What does it mean?

Often middle names evoke a smile or a chuckle. Some folks avoid embarrassment at their middle name by using only the initial. When my son attended Thomas W. Harvey High School, he became curious about that middle initial. So he asked what the "W" stood for. The teachers didn't know. The principal didn't know either, until he looked it up and discovered the "W" stands for Wadleigh. No wonder it was never written out.

So what does our middle name "evangelical" mean? It comes from a Greek word, *evangelion*, meaning good news. In the King James Version it was translated as Gospel, an old English word for "good tidings." What is the good news? It is the story of our rescue from the worst of troubles. We are lost sinners headed for death and hell, but Jesus saved us from that dark future by His sacrifice for us at the cross. His resurrection puts the stamp of truth on it. We can count on it.

Following cancer surgery, a friend of mine was thrilled to hear his surgeon rejoice, "I got it all! I got it all!" Jesus, after suffering the punishment of all our sins at His crucifixion, declared, "It is finished! I got it all!" All the killing power of the cancer of sin is gone, if we will admit our lost condition and put all our trust in Christ. This is what "evangelical" means. Pure good news, after hopelessly bad news.

Some form of the word *evangelion* appears in the New Testament 127 times. In sixty-three of these it appears either in a verb form, meaning "preach the Gospel," or with another verb meaning "proclaim." Do you see the implications of this? "Evangelical" means not only having the good news, but telling it to all the world, beginning where you are.

Therefore, in plain English our church's name should read, Zion "Telling the Good News" Lutheran. We dare not hoard and hide the best news ever, but share and spread it near and far. Are we living up to our middle name? Are you? Am I?

Lord, grant each of us zeal and power through Your Holy Spirit, so that telling the good news of Jesus will truly be our middle name and our highest priority. Amen.

Freeze!

During recess at our Bible school, the kids play a wild exciting game called Freeze! Here's how it's played.

Mark off a limited area, such as a basketball court. Appoint three out of the group of thirty or so to play the part of the Enemy. They can freeze any player by tagging them. Those who are tagged must stay frozen in the position they were in when touched by the Enemy. The goal of the Enemy is to freeze everyone. The other thirty players are the Free. They have the contrasting power to unfreeze people by touching them. When frozen players are tagged by a teammate, they can run again and set others free.

As the game begins, they are all off and running. The game continues until all the Free are frozen by the Enemy or the Enemy give up in exhaustion or the five minute time limit expires. Now, thirty ought to be able to defeat three. At first it seems that way. But, surprise! It seldom turns out that way. Usually all are frozen in a short time. Why? The reasons are a study in human nature and a commentary on lazy Christianity which fails to evangelize and disciple people.

1. The Enemy are more determined. Pride drives them to run and run.
2. The Free do not take the game as seriously. It's just a game.
3. The Free feel safety in numbers.
4. The Free spare themselves and don't run as hard. They take rests.
5. Some Free stand in a corner and don't risk getting involved until too late, when no one remains to set them free.
6. When they do risk getting involved, it is usually only to help a friend or relative. Then they retire again to a safe place.
7. Many of the Free allow a few aggressive kids to do most of the running and freeing, while they look on from safety.
8. They do not see the mission of "rescuer of all" as their personal calling.

Each of these eight points explains why Christians are often defeated. They rejoice in being free, but fail to recognize they have been set free by the Gospel to free others. So they play a self-centered, defensive game, and they lose. The surest way to stay free, to stay a saved Christian, is to be constantly moving in search of others whom we can touch and set free from the Enemy.

IGNITION

He will baptize you with the Holy Spirit and with fire. Matthew 3:11

A candle sheds no light,
a motor will not run,
a bullet will not fly,
a matchstick will not burn,
a rocket will not soar,
if there is not first of all
ignition.

Neither did the sun shine
till set ablaze by God
who flung it into space
to overcome the dark.
For Jesus is Himself
the very light of Life
eternal.

So my inner spirit,
a deep, death-dark dungeon,
knew no light, found no hope
till the Spirit of God—
the cross of Christ His torch—
lit the flame of new life
in my soul.

Now that I'm ignited
with Jesus in my heart,
O Lord, please make of me
an ever-burning bush
which never is consumed
while kindling flames of faith
left and right.

GUIDE TO THE SOUL-WINNER

1. Share, oh share, the good news—glad-ly! Tell with cour-age, "He's the Way";
2. Show all those who come to Je-sus What it means to trust this Way,
3. Then be faith-ful to dis-ci-ple Those whom God gives you to lead.
4. Al-le-lu-ia, Al-le-lu-ia, Al-le-lu-ia, Christ is Lord!

Hold up Je-sus as the Sav-ior, Ask God's Spir-it what to say;
Spir-it-filled to fol-low with us Near-er Je-sus ev-'ry day,
Ev-er teach-ing just like Je-sus Did the twelve A-pos-tles feed;
He's our joy and per-fect Sav-iour God-with-us in full ac-cord.

Make it plain and make it sim-ple So a child can un-der-stand,
Search-ing scrip-tures, answ'r-ing ques-tions, Pray-ing with un-ceas-ing joy;
'Til in turn they will be shar-ing All their new-found for-tune, too,
Lost we were, de-serv-ing noth-ing, Yet He's brought us back from hell;

Help each one to solve life's rid-dle By the nail marks in His hands.
Join-ing with all oth-er Chris-tians Sa-tan's strong-holds to de-stroy.
That their rich-es may not dwin-dle By their hoard-ing God's Good News.
Fa-ther's mer-cy, Je-sus' earn-ings, Spir-its' birth and all is well.

Text: Ottomar E. Bickel, 1972
Tune: John Zundel, 1870

ACTS 26:2 "I think myself happy, King Agrippa, because I shall answer for myself this day."

The Parachute

Jesus made an amazing claim about himself: "He that has the Son has life, he that has not the Son has not life, but the wrath of God abides on Him" (Jn. 3:36). Who could be that indispensable?

One Sunday I borrowed a sky-diver's parachute and wore it in the pulpit. How could a parachute preach a sermon? When you jump from a flying plane, you must be wearing a parachute to save your life. Picking out a soft-looking green pasture to land on will do no good. The ground and gravity combine to make a hard fact that will smash you.

When you and I die—as we surely will—and stand before God in the judgment, we need the Savior, Jesus Christ, to survive. The hard fact is that God is really holy and can't permit anyone into heaven who is not. We are not. We can no more be holy than we can fly. Every day we plummet closer to a jarring impact with the holy God.

A parachute is very carefully designed and constructed of sound material, in order to open up, catch the air, and slow one's speed for a safe landing.

God our Father, who loves us though we are wayward children, designed a Savior, made of divine material, who would meet the eternal laws and successfully save us from Adam's fall. The holy Jesus, who never sinned, let God lay on Him the sins of us all. At the cross He paid the dues of our sins. He rose from the tomb with victory over death for each of us. He said, "Because I live, you shall live also" (Jn. 14:19).

Of course, to be saved by a parachute, you have to put it on. So to be saved by Christ, you must wear Christ, consciously placing your trust in Him and letting Him take over your life. The Bible says, "They that have been baptized into Christ have put on Christ" (Gal. 3:27).

Merely knowing about a parachute is not enough. The most experienced parachute instructor will die as easily as an ignorant novice, if he jumps without a parachute. The jump to judgment before God comes at your death or at the Last Day, and neither is marked on the calendar.

Do you have Christ? Do you possess Him? Are you wearing Him? You may claim Him by confessing your sins today and strapping Him on by faith and wearing Him all the time.

When you wear Christ, He will show. People will ask about Him, just as if you were wearing a parachute all the time. Yes, you will find He is a burden, but He said, "My yoke is easy and My burden is light" (Mt. 11:30). When you are falling in death, plummeting toward Judgment Day, Christ doesn't weigh anything at all. Then He's as light as a feather and as handy as two wings.

Are You a Good Egg?

This is a heart-to-heart talk about a heart-to-heart relationship. I am referring to a true relationship with God through Christ. The Lord looks on the heart. The Lord knows the heart.

I hold an egg in my hand. "What is it," I ask?

Wondering why I would ask such a simple, obvious question, you reply, "An egg is an egg is an egg."

"Not so fast!" I say. "You had better inspect this 'egg is an egg' to know its true nature. It could be a true, fresh, fertile egg or it could be a phoney."

The same holds true for the man who calls himself a Christian. If I ask you, "What is a Christian?", you may say, "A Christian is a Christian."

Not so fast! What may God, who knows the heart, discover when he inspects someone who calls himself a Christian? Such a person could be any of the following:

1. A true, live, fertile egg—A born-again Christian, alive to God, trusting alone in Jesus, a reproductive witness for Christ. Or he could be—
2. A hard-boiled egg—A Christian who over time has become spiritually tough, proud and insensitive to God and people. Or he could be—
3. A rotten egg—Still dead in trespasses and sin. Not born again. Or he could be—
4. A hollow egg—Once a Christian, the insides now siphoned out by Satan (as a fox does). A mere show of a Christian. A hypocrite. Or he could be—
5. A petrified egg—Once a Christian now turned to stone, venerating the traditions. Having a form of godliness, but denying the power thereof. Or he could be—
6. A plastic egg—Never was an egg. Never was a Christian. Merely joined a church. Or he could be—

7. An infertile egg—A Christian, but not a witness, even though we were born again to reproduce by bringing others to Christ.

Here is the real issue: What am I? Am I a 'good' egg or a 'bad' egg? When we handle an egg and hold it before a bright light, we learn the truth about its nature. When we search our hearts with the light of Jesus and His Word, we will learn the truth about ourselves. What we all need to discover is that without God, every single one of us is a bad egg. We can only be cleansed of our rottenness by confessing our sin and trusting Christ and His cross for forgiveness.

Lord, help me to be honest with you and myself. Only by Christ's grace and the Spirit's power can I be a good egg, following in Christ's footsteps as His disciple and witness. Amen.

The Key of Life

Once while vacationing out west, I discovered we had left our second set of car keys at home. Since I like to fish in remote places, it was potentially very serious to be locked out of my vehicle with no help available for miles. So again and again, I clutched my keys in one hand while closing the car door.

Are you carrying the key of life? Not just any key will work. Only the one, right key will do. Since our sins condemn us, we need an escape key. Hold on tightly to the resurrected Jesus as your personal Savior. He said, "I have the keys of death and hell" (Rev. 1:18). By His death on the cross, He has prepared an escape route for each of us. He has the key.

During my western trip, I eventually had enough sense to make a second set of keys. What a relief it was to travel without the constant fear of getting locked out. When it comes to Jesus, there is no one to take His place. "I am the way... No one comes to the Father but by me" (Jn. 14:6). He has overcome death and brought life and immortality to us through the message of the cross (2 Tim. 1:10). With him, no one need live in fear of being locked up by death and hell.

Being rich and famous is no substitute for having Christ's key. On a Monday night football broadcast, Al Davis, owner of the

Oakland Raiders, said, "I like challenges. They are there to be met and overcome. But recently I've been intrigued with the challenge of death, and for that I have no answer." Before the actor Jackie Gleason died, he often expressed his fear of death. This fear is shared by many people.

The Bible says that without faith in Christ we are all lifetime slaves of the fear of death (Heb. 2:14). But when the Son sets you free, you are really free (Jn. 8:36). Like St. Paul, you can challenge death without fear, saying, "Death, where is your sting, grave where is your victory?... Thanks be to God who gives us the victory through our Lord Jesus Christ" (1 Cor. 15:55, 57).

Although they may never say it aloud, many people think, "First, I'll face the challenge of living today. Later on, I'll deal with the challenge of death." They fail to realize that this decision ruins the present moment as they must live with submerged fear of death. Why not face death right now and settle the matter once and for all?

Simply call upon Christ to unlock death's door for you. He died in your place, has paid for your sins, and will lift your guilt forever. Then you can live every day with a light heart, ready to meet God whenever He calls you from this world. Trusting in Christ, you hold the key to life in your hand.

Where Would I Go?

1. My dear Lord Jesus, if I did not have you,
Had not your heart's-blood bought the sinner's rescue,
Where would I, poorest of the whole world's wretched,
Turn to be blessed?

2. In my deep sorrow, where would I then go
To find a Savior with a heart that loves so?
You, Lord, only, give such true security.
Who else gives purity?

3. So let me thank you from my inmost spirit.
Sure hope you promised, brought me to believe it,
And into blood-saved company have led me
For all eternity.

4. How can I now keep silent and not tell this
To ev'ry lost one still without forgiveness?
Must I not share this hope with all those who lack it,
Through Thy good Spirit?

5. Must I not show this in my ev'ry action,
In all my dealings having true compassion,
Reflecting Jesus' love from within my being,
All men's need seeing?

Stanzas 1–3 are translated from the German hymn, "Ach Mein Herr Jesu," from the Liederperlen. Stanzas 4–5 by Ottomar E. Bickel

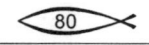

IMPROVING FISHING SKILLS

Fishers of souls need not be trapped at their present witnessing skill level. God is continually teaching us, so that we can advance, improve, and touch lives in ways which we were unable to earlier. To illustrate this point, let me describe my growth over the decades.

Beginnings. I began my pastoral career in 1942 at Christ Lutheran Church in White Cloud, Michigan. The first year I toiled like a dynamo, teaching eight different confirmation classes, calling youths and adults to trust in Christ and follow Him. Thirty-five people responded with faith, eleven of them adults who had never been baptized before. I felt good about that. Then the next adult confirmation class had only one adult. God was teaching me that He alone gives the increase.

Meanwhile, at Zion Lutheran Church, in Painesville, Ohio, someone read in the Synod's statistical yearbook about White Cloud's large adult confirmation class. So four Zion members made a trip to White Cloud to make my acquaintance. Before long, I received and accepted the call to be Zion's pastor. My tenure there began in February, 1947.

Remarkable growth occurred during the first two years in Painesville. In Zion's first fifty-six years, its membership had grown to 245. During my first two years there, 110 more people joined the congregation. Praise God!

However, as I look back on that time, I realize that I did most of the witnessing and failed to train and use my lay people to reach out to others. Many people are eager to assume that evangelism is the pastor's job, and I myself was tricked by this error.

Teaching others. Then came "Preaching, Teaching, Reaching" (PTR), an evangelism thrust of our denomination in the 1950s. I thought PTR would get more lay people involved. Initially it did. I organized 113 Zion members to participate in evangelistic calls and meetings. I'd never had that many people involved in evangelism before. But when I tried to duplicate this effort later on, the numbers dwindled to twenty-two, then seven, and finally just two—the members of my evangelism committee! The people simply found witnessing too difficult to do.

Several years went by. People were still coming to faith through my pastoral work. Zion helped plant several other churches in the region. Yet there remained a nagging, unfulfilled desire to involve more people. Sensing that my ministry was becoming a bit stale, I seriously considered taking a sabbatical during the summer of 1970. My plan was to move to Elko, Idaho, and work as a carpenter. I hoped this might help me establish common ground with unchurched people, so I could learn how to witness to them in a non-professional manner.

I still think it was a good idea, but I never took that sabbatical. Instead, during the next twenty-five years of my ministry, God led me to several evangelism-minded Christians from various churches. With their help I experienced great personal spiritual growth and the expansion of outreach in my congregation.

It started when I received an invitation to the Billy Graham School of Evangelism to be held in Knoxville, Tennessee in June of 1970. There I found hundreds of pastors from many denominations, all of them as eager as I was to have their members share the gospel. All of them also as frustrated as I was.

The main reason I went to Knoxville was to hear Rev. D. James Kennedy of Coral Ridge Presbyterian Church in Fort Lauderdale, Florida. I had heard about his Evangelism Explosion strategy, but I was skeptical. I suspected Kennedy was just a hot shot salesman. But at the School of Evangelism he came across as real and sincere. And his strategy was working—with three hundred lay people going out on evangelism calls every week.

Why did Kennedy's strategy work? Because he wasn't trying to train dozens of people all at once, as I had done with PTR. Instead, he taught just two people at a time. Discipled them slowly. Mentored them patiently. Finally, when they were competent and confident, they each would teach two others.

I went home and started doing the same thing. Slowly but surely, we at Zion started to see God using us—all of us, not just the pastor—to wake people up to the gospel. Over the next ten years, I also helped train about seventy area pastors in this method.

LEM. Another great influence on myself and Zion was Lutheran Evangelism Movement (LEM). For several years, they provided speakers for a week of renewal services at Zion. In particular, Pastor Herb Franz from St. Paul's Lutheran Church in Cloquet, Minnesota, was a great blessing to us. What a communicator! Herb wouldn't let an audience settle for a cold relationship with the church when what they needed was a warm faith relationship with Christ. Every night he would knock us down with the Law, and then lift us up with the Gospel. Zion grew mightily during the LEM weeks.

Most of the people associated with LEM were of Scandinavian and Finnish descent. I asked myself why they were so unlike some of the traditional German Lutheran churches. As I talked with LEM personnel I learned the answer.

The state churches in their homelands (especially in Norway and Finland) had a long history of revival movements during the 18th and 19th centuries. Providentially, these revival movements did not splinter off from the State Churches. Rather the revivals remained in the established church, thereby awakening, energizing, and revitalizing the state churches. Both pastors and lay preachers proclaimed Christ. People expressed their faith in original poetry and hymn tunes which still bless believers today.

When immigrants from these churches came to the United States, they brought with them these church customs which have continued to revitalize the churches they established here. All this explained to me why their descendents in the Lutheran Evangelism Movement appreciate both beautiful formal worship and informal, close-knit sharing of the faith.

Continued progress. Other evangelistic people and movements continued to influence us at Zion. I don't have time to tell you about the impact of Bill Bright and Campus Crusade, Dawson Trotman and the Navigators, Francis and Edith Schaeffer of L'Abri Fellowship, and the Great Commission Convocations of the Lutheran Church-Missouri Synod.

During the first half of my ministry, I was trying to do too much of it myself, thus making my job as a pastor more burdensome than it needed to be. Everything started improving when I learned to patiently disciple others and then trusted them and the Holy Spirit to do their ministry.

God is faithful. Over the years, I grew in my soul-winning skills, and my people grew in their witnessing skills.

So will you.

A Letter to Billy Graham

March 15, 1994

Dear Brother in Christ,

I have meant to write to you for forty years. We have so much in common. Jesus is our mutual Savior and friend. We are both Evangelicals—you a Baptist and I a Lutheran. We both believe the Bible is the true word of God, with a message everyone desperately needs to hear. You have served as a world evangelist and I as a parish pastor stressing evangelism and discipleship. We're both seventy-five years old. Our wives are named Ruth, and both are very helpful in our ministries. We both have Parkinson's disease, and we have known about it for five years. I pray for you to be able to continue your ministry.

I have been at Zion forty-seven years. We are praying and preparing for the Lord to bless the Northeast Ohio Crusade, coming on June 8-12. I have attended three of your crusades and accompanying evangelism conferences. The first one was in Knoxville, Tennessee in 1970. That week radically upgraded my outreach ministry. I was in my mid-forties and felt stymied about training lay people for personal evangelism. Dr. James Kennedy's lectures got me going with Evangelism Explosion. We have fifty people going out on calls every week. Many fantastic experiences have resulted.

In the Evangelism Museum at the Billy Graham Center in Wheaton, Illinois, I saw a display about the work of Dr. Walter A. Maier, first speaker of the Lutheran Hour. He was my professor at Concordia Seminary and a great inspiration to me as a preacher of the Gospel. It is said that years ago Dr. Maier once visited you when you were ill in the hospital in Chicago. Then at the time of his final illness, you called on him at the Lutheran hospital in St. Louis. Is this story accurate? I have always felt that God raised you up after Dr. Maier, as Elisha followed Elijah. I admire the striking simplicity, clarity, and moving force of your sermons. You reach plain folks and learned minds at the same time. You are an example and guide for me and for countless others.

I am glad to see Franklin stepping forward to help you. Thanks for your family photo sent to us last Christmas. We display it proudly. You are like one of the family for all of us.

We love you in Christ.
Ottomar E. Bickel

Sweet Harvest

As bees fly from the hive
   east, west, north, south, you too shall strive
   through all remaining daylight hours
   to search out and bring back nectar
   for the Beekeeper-Creator
     from within each bloom and flower.

"Receive the Holy Ghost
   to reach the souls of precious lost,"
   Christ commissioned the eleven.
They made their life's full endeavor
   to bring His love's costly treasure
     to golden honeycombs of heaven.

Disciples of today,
   under late, dark-red sunset rays,
   will you be worker bee or drone?
Spirit of God, stir up your hive
   to fly while hope is still alive
     to bring the last great harvest home.

6

DEVOTIONAL LIFE

Tested, Tempered, Triumphant

Why is my mind so much disturbed?
On all sides I feel the pressure
Of great demands to be observed,
No relenting and no leisure.
    Pressed to the wall and in despair,
    Who relieves my hurt and sorrow?
    My pleas—they vanish in the air.
    No response—today, tomorrow.

Yet God is there! He knows my need,
But waits and waits, my faith to test;
Not for Himself, but so I'll heed
The offer in His love to rest.
    He is enough! No matter how
    I feel deprived and lacking much.
    And when before His will I bow,
    I find rich healing in His touch.

Yes, Jesus has made peace with God.
And thus, while I believe in Him,
My soul, much burdened as I plod,
Will become more firm and trim.
    Then, when he who seeks to kill
    Attacks my spirit in the night,
    My tempered faith will last, until
    Through Christ I've conquered in the fight.

Prayer for a Worshipful Spirit

By Your Spirit,
Lord, help me
to worship You
in a spirit—

of remembering
of awareness
of thankfulness
of freshness
of caring
of enthusiasm
of abandonment
of fervency
of great joy
of adoration
of deep love
of loyalty
of treasuring
of admiration
of delight
of praise
of confession
of profession
of declaration
of proclamation
of commitment
of seeking
of finding
of dedication
of victory
of rejoicing
of wonder
of closeness

of willingness
of yieldedness
of surrender
of exaltation
of claiming
of believing
of anticipation
of hope
of faith
of excitement
of asking
of teachableness
of learning
of growing
of daring
of strength
of power
of wisdom
of sensitivity
of kindness
of meltedness
of softness
of flexibility
of renewal
of obedience
of love
of cheerfulness
of peace—

imitating Jesus
in every way,
every day,
and so live
in the Spirit.
Amen.

DEVOTIONAL LIFE · 87

JESUS, RAPTURE OF MY HEART

1. Je - sus, rap - ture of my heart, Sweet - est Je - sus!
2. Con - stant - ly I think of You, Pre - cious Sav - ior!
3. Lead me to your pas - tures wide: I am hun - gry!
4. None as beau - ti - ful as You, My be - lov - ed!
5. I am sick! Come heal your friend: Make me strong - er!

My soul's hap - pi - ness You are, Sweet - est Je - sus!
And crave no - thing else to do, Pre - cious Sav - ior!
Springs of wa - ter, please, pro - vide: I am thirs - ty!
No one friend - li - er than You, My be - lov - ed!
I'm worn out and at the end: Wait no long - er!

For my life, a fresh, new start,
Al - ways to be near - er to You,
Let me lie down by your side,
None as sweet to me as You,
When I die, sweet com - fort send,

Sweet - est Je - sus, Je - sus, Sweet - est Je - sus!
Pre - cious Sav - ior, Je - sus, Pre - cious Sav - ior!
Rest of wea - ry, Je - sus, Rest of wea - ry!
Sweet - est Lov - er, Je - sus, Sweet - est Lov - er!
My con - sol - er, Je - sus, my Con - sol - er!

Translated from "Jesus Meines Herzens Freud" (252 Lutherisehes Gesangbuch) by O.E. Bickel

Holy Land Morning

At 4 A.M., I woke up with a strange feeling. "Where am I?" I wondered.

My weary mind slowly pieced together the last thirty hours. An airplane. The Atlantic. The Mediterranean. Tel Aviv at midnight. An hour-long, uphill bus ride. Then Jerusalem, alight by night. A hotel in the Kidron Valley, near the walls of the Old City. To bed by 2 A.M.

Ruth and I never dreamed we would visit the Holy Land. I had always said, "We have the Bible to tell it all. It's true and it's enough." And it is. Then in 1972 on our 25th anniversary at Zion, the congregation generously presented us with a gift trip. The next day, I heard on the radio: "War may break out in Israel at any moment." At a bon voyage fellowship dinner, I teased them about their plan to get rid of me.

Now, lying in pitch darkness at 4 A.M., what a warm sensation to slowly comprehend we were in the Holy City!

My waking prayer time was rich. How blessed I felt as I pictured Jesus rising before dawn for prayer and communion with His Father. By way of His cross, I was permitted the same privilege.

Then a sound broke the stillness. It couldn't be. A rooster had crowed in anticipation of the dawn. I was spellbound. Then again, clearer and louder. No mistaking it.

In a place not far from here, but so long ago, Peter heard Christ's sad prophecy fulfilled. Long ago became right now for me. The cock crowing made me think back to my silences and evasions over the years, my weak testimony and cowardly heart, and even sinful chiming in with the world. All these amounted to denial of my Savior.

Then I felt the kind eyes of Jesus turned on me. I confessed my sins, and the Lord washed my spirit with tears of remorse and repentance. There in the dark before dawn, the Lord helped me pray for His Holy Spirit to give me greater courage and power to confess Him, who had hallowed this place forever with His blood and death and resurrection.

God was waiting to meet me early that first morning in the Holy Land. So He awaits us every morning.

With Jesus by the Sea

MARK 4:1-2

How wonderful to be
   with Jesus by the sea,
   and there to sit upon the shore
   His words and person to adore,
   as from a ship he preached to me.

Green hills of Galilee
   as far as eye can see.
   Sky-blue water, calm and clear,
   a place now made forever dear.
   Had you been there you would agree.

From out the ship He taught,
   like fish the hearers caught;
   deep mysteries made very plain,
   by simple parables explained
   to eager list'ners wrapped in thought.

As through that sea there rolled
   the Jordan waters cold,
   fresh from Mt Hermon's crystal snow;
   so truth from GOD He gave to know,
   in all the things He said and told.

Note: We went by ship across the Sea of Galilee on a calm day, with hardly a ripple on the water. Then our guide called our attention to a current passing through the sea, a current caused by the Jordan River. Reflecting on this phenomenon, I composed this poem.

God Be with You Till We Meet Again

Jesus sweetens the bitter taste of parting.

My father was both pastor and school teacher at Christ Lutheran Church in Birch Run, Michigan, where I was born. School was conducted in the church next to the parsonage. He had all eight grades in one room. It was a warm and wonderful Christian school.

I experienced my first Christian parting when my father accepted a call to another parish. They say, "Parting is such sweet sorrow." But on the last day of school all the children sang a hymn which brought sweet comfort.

> God be with you till we meet again.
> With His counsels guide, uphold you.
> With His sheep securely fold you.
> God be with you till we meet again.
>   Till we meet, Till we meet,
>   Till we meet at Jesus' feet.
> God be with you till we meet again.

Forty-seven years later, Ruth and I were on a Boeing 747 as it prepared for landing at New York's Kennedy airport. On board were 475 Holy Land pilgrimage tourists. Seated near us were the forty new friends we had made while touring together by bus. For ten days we had walked where Jesus walked, prayed where Jesus prayed, and sung where Jesus sang.

The pastor who led our group asked if I would lead a closing song. Ruth suggested, "God Be With You Till We Meet Again." After the first few words, those around us joined in, and by the second line all 475 pilgrims were singing with strong voices and fervent emotion. Knowing we would soon scatter, we comforted each other with the prospect of the sure, future rendezvous described in the chorus: "Till we meet at Jesus feet."

In the hush following the song, I reflected back to that boyhood parting and the many since. A heavenly reunion awaits all who trust in the crucified and risen Savior, Jesus Christ, at their journey's end. That sure hope sweetens every parting no matter what the circumstances.

DEVOTIONAL LIFE   91

ONLY JESUS

1. Fa - ther hear me As I pray to Thee.
2. Make me to be still, With Thy Spir - it fill

Give me eyes to see I've lived self - ish - ly.
All my heart un - til I live in Thy will.

Thou hast made me And re - deemed me.
Just to praise Thee, On - ly please Thee,

Through Thy Ho - ly Son We are made as one.
All through Je - sus, On - ly Je - sus.

Text: Ottomar E. Bickel
Music: Prelude in C minor (Opus 28 No. 20) by Frederic Chopin

Needed: Prayer Warriors

"For our struggle is not against flesh and blood, but against the rulers, against the authorities, against the powers of this dark world and against the spiritual forces of evil in the heavenly realms.... And pray in the Spirit on all occasions with all kinds of prayers and requests." Eph. 6:12, 18a

Prayer is volunteering.
Prayer is enlisting.
Prayer is respect.
Prayer is discipline.
Prayer is work.
Prayer strengthens.
Prayer takes time and patience.
Hurry up, pray, and wait.

Prayer takes energy.
Prayer is exercise of the soul
Prayer is training.
Prayer is power at the cross.
Prayer is claiming promises.
Prayer is believing God.
Prayer is believing His Word.
Hurry up, pray, and wait.

Prayer is dedication to a cause.
Prayer flies its flag.
Prayer is carrying our cross.
Prayer is stockpiling God's power.
Prayer is defense.
Prayer attacks hell.
Hurry up, pray, and wait.

Prayer takes perseverance!
Prayer leads to victory!
Needed: Prayer Warriors Now!
Hurry up, pray, and wait!

DEVOTIONAL LIFE   93

PRAISE GOD

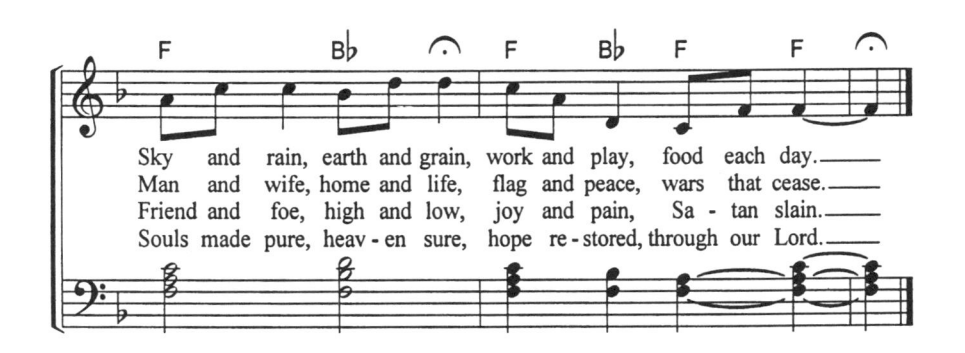

1. Praise God for— sun and light, moon and night,
2. Praise God for— prayer and psalm, Dad and Mom,
3. Praise God for— health and zest, ease and test,
4. Praise God for— fear dis-pelled, truth up-held,

Sky and rain, earth and grain, work and play, food each day.
Man and wife, home and life, flag and peace, wars that cease.
Friend and foe, high and low, joy and pain, Sa-tan slain.
Souls made pure, heav-en sure, hope re-stored, through our Lord.

Words and melody by Ottomar E. Bickel
Harmonization by Ruth-Esther Hillila-Bickel

FOR DEEP THIRST

"As the deer pants for streams of water,..." Psalm 42:1

So like a mountain stream—
   where waters flow cool and clean,
   and thirsty deer tiptoe to the edge—
is Jesus Christ refreshing
to minds and spirits
parched and arid.

How Deep Is the Ocean?

"... and to know this love that surpasses knowledge..." Ephesians 3:19

What depths of love did it require
when Christ was on the cross
and bore the blame and shame
of the whole world?

We know as much of it as a boy
knows of the depths of the ocean
from standing on the shore
skipping stones across the surface.

We know as much as a girl
knows of the depths of the ocean
from testing the water with her toes
as a wave skims up the sand.

What these children may have learned,
we in proportion comprehend
of the depth of the love of Christ
which surpasses all our knowledge.

O Lord, What a Morning!

"Very early in the morning, while it was still dark, Jesus got up, left the house and went off to a solitary place, where he prayed." Mark 1:35

I too, rose up early, just before dawn. My eagerness to explore a new place was my alarm clock. Strapping on my camera and carrying my tape recorder for the bells, I started up the mountain at a brisk walk. Where was this? Weissbad, Switzerland, half way up Mount Santis in the Alps.

Soon I turned onto a private, blacktopped farm road which angled up the mountain slope. The narrow roadway became a paved path, winding yet higher. The sun now burst over the mountain upon the native scene of homes and farms on mountain slopes and a neat valley with three villages strung along the stream. A toy-sized train chugged through the valley. From distant steeples bells rang out every quarter hour.

I praised the Lord, and He led me into deep thoughts. I thanked God for the Savior and Holy Spirit within me and for the dear ones filling my life. My wife still asleep in the cozy farm house lodging. Children and grandchildren, family, friends, and congregation back home across an ocean. And loved ones already home with God beyond earth's horizons.

A path well worn by flocks invited me to go higher and higher. I passed a sheep shelter and continued upward. My camera shutter clicked steadily as the glorious sunlight scaled down from the heights and swept over the panorama.

Then I saw it! To the southwest a whole new valley emerged out of the one I had been viewing. Before it had appeared as only a narrow cleft. But I had hiked so far and gone so high that I could now peer into it. The sun revealed a shining stream and lofty green pastures stretching beyond my power to see—and promising more.

God, my daily Teacher, spoke to my heart, "And so will heaven be, my child. When earth's valley ends with death and seems to be all there is, by resurrection sunrise rays you will view another and a better Vista. There the Lamb your Shepherd will feed you and lead you to fountains of living waters" (Rev. 7:17).

As I looked back down the sheep trail I had followed, only a few feet below me was a large sheep trough hewn out of stone by the shepherds, brimming and running over with fresh water from a mountain spring. Even at this distant height the shepherd supplies his sheep.

My prayers were precious at that quiet place. I did not want them to end. God's companionship touched my senses and arrested all other thoughts. When the church bells chimed again, I recalled the song "The Lamb Is My Shepherd" [which appears on the following pages]. So I stood beside the water trough, gazing up that shining new valley and sang the hymn with a strength of faith and heart's abandon only God's Spirit can give.

O Lord, what a morning! My photos and these words fall far short of telling what I saw and heard and felt and learned. Once again Jesus had shown me the preciousness of dawn—echo of Easter, foretaste of heaven's new day.

THE LAMB IS MY SHEPHERD

Andante

1. God of true light In whom is no night Ev-er lead me. In my dark night By Christ-mas star-light Ev-er guide me To the man-ger There to pon-der The great won-der. So like Mar-y And the shep-herds I'll re-mem-ber.

2. Cross-marked Je-sus, Ris-en Je-sus, Make me ev-er Free from sin stain Safe in faith's claim Doubt-ing nev-er. Pre-cious Sav-ior My Re-deem-er, Live with-in me. No more my will, On-ly Your will, Yours the glo-ry.

3. Ho-ly Spir-it Sent from Je-sus And the Fa-ther My con-vert-er New heart giv-er And truth teach-er Fill my be-ing With Your pow-er Have Your way Ev-er see-ing On-ly Je-sus 'Til that day.

DEVOTIONAL LIFE 97

4. Lamb, my shepherd, Lead me up to Heaven's mountains. There await me Lush, green pastures And fresh fountains. Hallelujah, Praise the Father, Praise the Son,⎯ Hallelujah, Praise the Spirit, The vict'ry's won.⎯ Hallelujah, Praise the Father, Praise the Son, Hallelujah, Praise the Spirit, All ever One.

Words and Melody: Ottomar E. Bickel
Harmonization: Hilbert Collins

In Sync with God

"Yet not what I will, but what you will." Mark 14:36

The will of God and my will must flow together,
As one.
I ask not why or whether,
His will be done!

The thoughts of God and my thoughts align
To rhyme;
My crude self-serving refined
To the sublime!

The plans of God and my plans must fully match,
All ways.
I may neither add nor scratch.
His blueprint stays!

So have Your way with me, Savior, Immanuel,
My head.
You, dear Lord, be the needle,
I the thread!

Such perfect harmony of life I had not known,
Till now.
A true peace with God I own,
With joy I bow!

WHAT I SEE BY THE SEA

The view from my home on Lake Erie.

How do I turn
   a picture panorama
   viewed from my porch rocker
   into a poem of praise?

What my eyes now enclose
   from periphery to periphery
   are greens and blues
   of many hues
   in earth and sea and sky

The foreground
   of lawn and flowers and hedge
   yields to shoreline trees
   and boundless expanses
   of azure background

The sun, brilliant and cheerful
   highlights sails and surf
   white caps and gulls
   bathers and anglers
   and bleached breakwall rocks

Near the center
   a sturdy lighthouse towers
   its lamp still shines by night
   to guide the lost

Add two freighters heading west;
   one close up and looming large
   the other on the distant rim
   in miniature

The horizon
   sharply etched
   God draws straight lines
   freehand

The air washed clean by recent rain
   all is in sharp focus
   from left to right
   from front to back
   from finite to infinite
   for eyes of mind and spirit

Lord, my Maker and my Saviour,
   may my heart's thanks and praise
   match your art and grace

REASON TO FOLLOW

"Follow me." Matthew 4:19

Lord Jesus, I will go where you go.

You are the Breath of my life.
You are the Wisdom of my mind.
You are the Ransom of my soul.
You are the Sun of my day.
You are the Star of my night.
You are the Harmony of my family.
You are the Head of the church.
You are the Ruler of all nations.
You are the Creator of the world.
You are the Spring of the universe.
You are the King of heaven.
You are the Lord of all.

So, it makes sense, Lord Jesus—
Where You go, I will go.

Family and Nation

A Wedding Benediction

To the tune of "Bless This House"

Bless these friends who wed today,
Bless them, Lord, in every way.
Bless their lives with daily joy,
Let not storms their calm destroy.
Bless the home in which they dwell,
Drawing love from Thy deep well.
Bless their souls that they may be
Ever trusting, Lord, in Thee.

Bless their day so shining bright
Made by Thee for their delight.
Bless the loved ones gathered here,
Each one in his own way dear.
Bless our Savior, who made sure
By His cross, that we be pure.
Thank Thee, Lord, that now we stand
In the hollow of Thy hand.

Bless us all that one day we
May dwell, O Lord, with Thee.

Marvelous Marriage Mathematics

Marriage is as simple as
$$2 + 2 = 4$$

or rather as
$$1 + 1 = 2$$

Well, actually it should become
$$1 + 1 = 1$$

That's the way God intended in the beginning,
Except sin often divides and makes it
$$2 \div 1 = 2$$

The solution is simple.
Add one more—Christ.
He unites.
$$1 + 1 + 1 = 1$$

Almost as mysterious and marvelous
As the Holy Trinity, isn't it?

Like Two Left Feet

"Male and female he created them." Genesis 1:27

Chauvinism? Creates schism, 'me-first' isms.
Women's lib? What a fib! God didn't ad lib.

Two right feet will defeat, make you stumble.
Two left feet will compete, make you bumble.
If to be right or to be left each will resign,
Marriage fits opposites by God's design.
Step side by side without pride, not defiant,
Taking turns as each learns love is pliant.

For accord, see the Lord in the other.
Put Christ first, by love serve one another.
Jack is he. Jill is she. Christ balanced well
Our relation in creation. With Him excel.

Precious Appreciation

Hard-working and depressed,
  a woman answered the door.
A bouquet of flowers—
  "We appreciate you," the note said.
  "You are a wonderful wife and mother."
Her depression dissolved
  Amid tears of joy.

"Well done!" is a basic daily requirement
  of the soul.
Let's compliment others, lifting their spirits.
  Lord Jesus, let me start with you:
  "Well done! You saved a wretch like me."

Love That Never Fails

In their retirement years, my uncle and aunt, Emil and Agnes Bickel, taught mentally disabled people at a home in Perry County, Missouri. One day a doctor at that facility told them about the most amazing medical case he had ever seen.

Being the county coroner, he was called to examine the body of a 38-year old man who had died at home. What he saw made no sense at all. He could not find a single scar or evidence of scar tissue on the man's back or legs. The skin was undamaged and normal, like a child's. Why was the doctor so mystified?

The man he examined had been both mentally disabled and severely crippled, so helpless that he "could not brush a fly from his nose." Since childhood he had been a bed-patient in his mother's home, and all these years she had cared for her son herself.

"Such patients," the doctor said, "are commonly plagued by bed sores, which leave ugly red scars and welts when they heal. Imagine how many thousand times his mother-nurse lovingly turned his body, changed his position, and gave baths and massages to stimulate circulation. How regularly, like clock-work, she must have done it to achieve this perfect result. What faithfulness! I marvel at the extreme mother-love demonstrated in the unblemished skin of that man."

So must we marvel at the love of our heavenly Father. For He makes it possible that at the end of a life marred by sin, every believer in Christ will appear before Him without a single blemish, scar, or mark of the wrongs we have done (Eph. 5:27).

By means of the immeasurable love of Jesus, who bore our sins on the cross and washed us in His own blood, we will be without stain. "The blood of Jesus, God's Son, purifies us from every sin" (1 Jn. 1:7).

By the faithful care of the Holy Spirit, who brings us to Christ and keeps us in faith through all the years, we will, after examination by a holy God, be found as unscarred as a new born baby. "How great is the love the Father has lavished on us, that we should be called children of God!"(1 Jn. 3:1).

"You'll See Adam before I Will"

"Because I live, you also will live." John 14:19

We sat in the big rocking chair by our picture window overlooking the harbor at sunset. Lake Erie mirrored the pastel hues of the sky.

"What an artist God is!" I said to my six-year old grandson sitting on my lap. Although it was dusk, the colors persisted as we rocked in the quiet and watched.

The boy stirred and said, "You know, Grandpa, I can hardly wait till I see Adam." He referred to his little brother. After being so eagerly awaited through the previous summer and fall, Adam had lived only one brief hour. At the wintry grave site on a hill near their farm house, we had all commended frail, little Adam to His Savior, Jesus.

"Grandpa, I'm not afraid to die anymore now that I believe I'll see Adam again in heaven."

"Those who trust in Jesus don't need to be afraid," I said. It was very quiet as we sat for a long time and looked and thought.

He stirred again, "Grandpa, you'll probably get to see Adam before I will, won't you?"

I pondered his calculations and said, "Probably."

The six-year old continued to ponder the mystery of God. "My daddy said, 'When Jesus was on the cross and died, He was God and man at the same time. We can't understand it, but it's true.' Is that right, Grandpa?"

"That's right, son." I made a mental note never to underestimate a child's grasp of theology.

We went to bed. As he lay next to me in the dark, he talked more and more about God and Adam and his own life in the future, as though a deep spring had opened and kept bubbling up. I answered many questions. Even though I became very sleepy, I hated to halt the flow of thoughts and questions.

Prior to his arrival for a few days of vacation with us by the lake, I had prayed, "Lord, while my dear grandson is here let me talk to him about You."

My prayer was answered with an evening I will treasure always.

Prayer for the Family

1. God, Fa-ther bless our home, Who for our sins a-toned With your own Son
2. Bind up all wounds and heal Heart-hurts and help us kneel In ear-nest prayer.
3. Give fa-thers, mo-thers love Of heav'nly things a-bove, To lead the way

Cleanse us from love-less wrong. Make ev'-ry home-bond strong.
Show us where we're at fault, Bring quar-rels to a halt;
In-to your Ho-ly Word, Which peace and hope af-fords.

Let each know he be-longs, Our fam'ly one.
Our speech, grace, mixed with salt, Of you a-ware.
That all may serve the Lord, Till that great day. A-men!

WORDS: Ottomar E. Bickel, 1981
MUSIC: "Thesaurus Musicus," 1740

AMERICA
6.6.4.6.6.6.4.

I have no greater joy THAN TO HEAR that my children walk in the truth. III JOHN 1:4

His Banner over Us Is Love

All nations have a flag. America has a flag with stars and stripes. Canada's flag has a maple leaf. The Mexican flag is red, green and white. Is there a flag for the Kingdom of God? Yes. Song of Songs 2:4 says, "His banner over me is love." That's the Christian flag. Love. God's love. It is a flag to honor and a flag to die for.

Flags have meanings and promise something. The American flag promises freedom, and many refugees from around the world will say it is true. But the flags and nations of earth never live up to all they promise. However, God's flag of love does live up to its promises. High over the heavenly Jerusalem flies a flag of perfect love. How the harassed and weary of this earth long to see it. Then we will be fully and forever free.

Love. This simple word includes all that God is, for God is love. Amid apparent defeat, the flag of love flew in victory on the cross of Calvary. "Greater love has no one than this, that he lay down his life for his friends" (Jn. 15:13). Christ's love has set us free.

Patriots revere their country by flying their flag. Christians stand up for Jesus by displaying the flag of love. "By this all men will know that you are my disciples, if you love one another" (Jn. 13:35).

You are invited to enlist in Christ's army. He came to seek and to save that which was lost. He met and overcame the enemy that held us captive. Whenever Christians join a church they are enlisting in the army of Jesus Christ, in order to help liberate all people from Satan's oppressive dictatorship.

Are you a Christian by choice or because of social pressure? Are you a volunteer or draftee? God is looking for volunteers.

In 1969, my son-in-law, Jim Crawford, had just graduated from Ohio State University with an agriculture degree. Although he was eager to begin work on his family's dairy farm, another duty called him. He joined the U. S. Marines and served a stint in Vietnam. He volunteered because he loved America and felt he owed it to his country.

Our present armed forces are all volunteers. The government feels it is better served by loyal, career-minded volunteers then by draftees who see themselves as victims of chance. Likewise Jesus, the Captain of the army of salvation, desires volunteers who are honored to serve, not draftees under duress. That's why He does not recruit us by 'Shanghai' force, but by the winsome invitation of the cross, where He loyally gave His life for us while we were still

God's enemies. Having brought us back to safety in His kingdom of love, the banner that now flies over us is His love.

Out of personal conviction and faith in Jesus, may you pledge allegiance to this flag. Under it may you serve with distinction against every evil foe and for every noble cause as a career soldier of the cross.

Primary Election

An election faces you every day. A selection must be made based on your convictions. It is a primary election, not because it is a preliminary vote, but because it is of primary importance. It is a national election, because everyone must decide. Your vote makes a difference, both today and forever.

BALLOT

Vote for 1 in each pair.

__ Wisdom
__ Folly

__ God's will
__ My will

__ God
__ False gods

__ Others
__ Self

__ Truth
__ Lies

__ Christ's holiness
__ My supposed worthiness

__ Good
__ Evil

__ Light
__ Darkness

__ The 10 Commandments
__ Majority opinion

__ Hope
__ Despair

__ Obedience
__ Disobedience

__ Life
__ Death

__ Godliness
__ Ungodliness

__ Heaven
__ Hell

The Closing of the American Mind

Do you have an open mind or a closed mind? You can't pour anything into a corked bottle. You can't teach a closed mind. Not even the truth can enter.

In *The Closing of the American Mind*, Allan Bloom examines the American college scene. His study begins with these words, "There is one thing a professor can be absolutely sure of: almost every student entering the university believes, or says he believes, that truth is relative" (Simon & Schuster, 1987, p. 25).

Most university students believe truth is flexible. They think truth can be shifted to suit the latest opinions. That sounds like an open mind but is really just the opposite. Truth as a dependable absolute is ruled out from the start. That's a closed mind. Truth and morality are only "personal preference." If everybody is right nobody is right. If every viewpoint is equally valuable, no viewpoint is valuable.

The modern view is the opposite of God's Word, which claims that truth is absolute, established and unchanging.

Thank God, He has absolutes. Praise God, right and wrong exist. We can protest all we want, but human beings have built-in absolutes. Guilt is real because law is real and sin is real. That's why lie detectors work.

An agnostic scientist said to me one evening, "If I can't put something in a test tube and examine it, it isn't real."

At that very moment, his two-year old daughter was hugging his knees, so I asked, "Does she love you?"

He smiled.

I asked, "You can't put that love in a test tube. So, is it real?"

He made no reply.

Many ridicule the Bible, although they have never read it. Christianity welcomes and deserves testing. Do you know what Jesus said and did? Can you claim an open mind if you have never read God's Word yourself and examined it's teachings?

Let me tell you another desperately needed absolute. We have a Savior who died for our guilt and canceled it, so that we can be absolutely sure of being saved, forgiven the moment we confess our sins and trust in Christ.

Knowing Him renews the mind. He is the final Truth.

CIVIL WAR II

"Righteousness exalts a nation, but sin is a disgrace to any people."
Proverbs 14:34

With our allies America won the "hot" war—World War II—against godless Nazism. After forty years of tension with Russia and Communism, we have apparently won the Cold War. The Iron Curtain and the Wall are gone.

Meanwhile, are we winning the current war in our own nation? I call it "Civil War II." It isn't a division of North and South, but a moral war against godlessness, lawlessness, immorality and self-indulgence. The two sides are: (1) those who know and trust God through Christ; and (2) those who do not know God and trust themselves.

After atheistic Communism failed in the Soviet empire are we becoming a godless nation, even losing our religious freedom? It appears we are headed that way. What a tragic twist of history.

Many in media and leadership positions are blind to the degeneration of virtues and defend each step downward as freedom. No wonder the Bible says "the god of this age [Satan] has blinded the minds of unbelievers, so that they cannot see the light of the gospel of the glory of Christ" (2 Cor. 4:4).

Christians, young and old, let's fight for the future of America. We begin the battle with prayer.

> *God, our Father, thank You for the gift of this free country, the United States of America. Thanks for the good You have done in the world through this unique nation. With joy we sing, "This land is my land," knowing full well "this land is Your land."*
>
> *Now help us come to grips with the growing internal problems of America and oppose the evil attacking us from within like a cancer. Your Word and counsel reveals it to be just plain sin.*
>
> *Holy Spirit, please alert every Christian to the key role he or she must play to bring about healing, so that Americans may repent, trust Christ, and be spiritually and morally strong. Dear Lord, begin with me. Amen.*

FAMILY AND NATION   111

There Is a Way, America

(Ref.) There is a way, A-me-ri-ca to heal this sin-sick land;
There is a way, A-me-ri-ca, just take the Saviour's hand.

Fine

If we will turn to Je-sus and ask Him to for-give;
If we turn back to Je-sus, the Fa-ther's love-gift Son,

D.C. Refrain

His cross will sure-ly heal us, He died that we might live.
His love will so u-nite us that we will be as one.

RIGHTEOUSNESS EXALTS A NATION BUT SIN IS A REPROACH TO ANY PEOPLE. PROVERBS 14:34

WORDS: Ottomar E. Bickel, 1988
MUSIC: Traditional Spiritual

BALM IN GILEAD
Irregular Meter

8 Heaven, Our Home

Nearer Home

I am old
   And I am glad.
It's pure gold
   And I'm not sad.

Nearer home,
   The goal in sight.
Angels, come.
   I've fought the fight.

The body fails
   But fears abate.
Faith prevails.
   Content I wait.

Till the end
   I'll point the Way
For lost friends
   Who've gone astray.

Christ within
   Fills my cup.
Freed from sin,
   I now look up—

Till Jesus comes.

THE AGONY AND THE ECSTASY OF AGING

Excerpts from a sermon delivered at age 72.

My dear aging friends—of all ages—are you afflicted with gerontophobia? That is the fear of getting old.

I've been wanting to preach on this subject for some time. All the while I've been aging and you've been aging. So I decided to go ahead before I was too old to preach and you too old to hear me.

In Psalm 37:25 David said, "I was young and now I am old." That was quick. The truth is, from the moment we are born we all are aging in a constant countdown.

Even at age seventy-two, I still am amazed I am no longer young. It's quite a shock when for the first time you hear yourself referred to as old. I was in my early sixties out for a walk on the beach, when from a distance I heard a conversation in which I was referred to as an "old man." The exact words were, "That old man over there is Pastor Bickel." No mistaking who was meant.

This shocking report was confirmed just two days later. While I was waiting at a stop light, a car full of young people pulled alongside—windows open, radio blaring. Then one of them loudly referred to the "old man in the next car" as though I were deaf. The light changed. They roared away. I looked around, and the only car in sight was mine. No mistaking who was meant.

So lets talk about the agony and ecstasy of aging. Agony sounds right. Ecstasy sounds unlikely. Gray hair, wrinkles, balding, getting winded easily, flab, and paunch are early signs of our decline. People fight aging with hair color, lotions and potions, diet and exercise, hair pieces and wigs, makeup and face lifts, all to no avail. Retirement years are often repair years, as we replace our worn out body parts for better models available in organ banks. Agonies mount as more and more repair are needed on the old car—I mean carcass.

This is why we don't like the look of old age, we don't like the feel of old age, we don't like the prejudice against old age, and we don't like the outcome of old age. "The young may die, the old must die."

Brain cells die from birth on. That's medical knowledge. Sin is with us from birth and is the cause of aging and death. That's spiritual knowledge. "The wages of sin is death" (Rom. 6:23).

Because the specter of death looms over life and glooms our days, the ecstasy of aging is not found primarily in retirement, leisure, fishing, golf, vacations, cruises, spas, and super senior communities. The ecstasy of aging is found in something deeper, richer, sweeter, brighter, surer, and best of all—permanent. The ecstasy of aging is this: to have Jesus, the victor over the grave, as your personal deliverer from death.

I'm so glad that Easter isn't over—but ever. By its very nature, the resurrection of Jesus Christ is constant and eternal. It is the atomic power core of Christianity. Are you tapping into that source of spiritual energy and courage?

Unbelievers fail to do so and live in fear. In the ballad "Ole Man River" a Mississippi River dock worker sings:

> I'm feared of livin'
> and skeered of dyin'
> but Ole Man River
> he just keeps rollin' along.

Without the risen Christ that's all there is. Time just keeps rollin'—and we are feared and skeered. That is agony. But the angel said at the empty grave of Jesus, "Do not be afraid.... he has risen, just as he said" (Mt. 28:5-6). If by faith you tap into that source of fearlessness, you will know the ecstasy of living, no matter what age you are.

Dr. Norman Vincent Peale tells of a sick call he made on a dying Christian woman. He asked how she was. With a rare and beautiful smile, she said, "Spiritually I'm all right and mentally also. Physically, I may as well tell you, I'm going to die." Her eyes showed great serenity. She was like a person getting ready for a long, beautiful journey. There was no craven fear, only trust. No agony, only ecstasy.

"I wanted to see you, Pastor," she explained, "not because I lacked comfort, but to urge you to go on preaching Christ's message of hope and faith. Keep on inviting people to receive Jesus Christ and maintain close companionship with Him, He will help them in every way. He is so close to me. I have no fear of life; I have no fear of death."

With such faith even the final years, despite problems and eventual death, can be the very best. The Lord promises, "The righteous will flourish like a palm tree.... They will still bear fruit in old age, they will stay fresh and green, proclaiming, 'the Lord is upright, he is my Rock, and there is no wickedness in him'" (Ps. 92:12, 14,-15). As you ponder this marvelous promise, there is no mistaking who is meant. God offers His forgiveness and care to you, no matter what your age. So as you ponder the brevity of life, may you often pray like this:

Lord, my God, prepare me for all of life, but most of all, prepare me for the last miles, that I may not falter or fall before crossing the finish line. Grant me victory through Christ who strengthens me. Through Him I can do all things, including facing death with faith in my Savior God. Amen.

AUGUSTA VEDRA

Augusta Vedra was a member of my church in Painesville, Ohio. Due to a strong desire for God's word, she memorized many Bible passages. In her later years, she became partially blind. Despite her visual disability, her knowledge of Scripture and delight in the Lord made her an inspiration to me and to everyone who knew her. Augusta's spiritual vision was 20/20. When she went to be with the Lord, I penned these lines.

When God takes home those who trust Christ fully,
There is no sadness. They have won out
And overcome.

This child of God yearned to hear God calling,
And is home at last. No questions left—
She is at peace.

Her eyes undimmed
See splendors we have not.
Her ears unstopped
Hear God's great voice.

She is content.
Her spirit with God
Is living,
In Jesus' care
Lacks nothing.

How do we know this?
God cannot lie!

Fountain of Youth

Is there a fountain of youth? Ponce de Leon looked for one in Florida. To no avail. Thousands of present-day people look for one by moving to Florida. To no avail. Don't get me wrong. Florida is a nice place. I winter there myself. But amid all its attractions, you won't find the fountain of youth.

Sin, aging, and death inevitably follow each other in order. Yet, through Jesus Christ, we can have a youthful outlook on life, and on death. Because Jesus paid the debt of our sins, He has brought life and immortality to light through the gospel (2 Tim. 1:10). Death is merely a doorway to heaven for those who believe in Christ. Life has purpose and meaning, because our heavenly future is secure through Christ.

But what if I get weak and sick or helpless and senile? The Lord promises, "Even to your old age and gray hairs I am he, I am he who will sustain you. I have made you and I will carry you; I will sustain you and I will rescue you" (Is. 46:4).

But what about loneliness? As friends die or move away, I might become isolated and lonely. Those who draw close to their heavenly Father find that He is permanent—a forever Father.

The very word "father" demands that. He says we are His children. If God had made us only to let us grow old and then toss aside like a broken toy, then He would be a toy maker, not a Father. Where can you rent a child for a year? Nowhere. Fatherhood is permanent. In the Psalms God repeatedly describes us as His children and Himself as our faithful Father.

Once we have been reconciled to the Father through repentance and trust in Christ's salvation, we become children in His forever family.

> There is a fountain filled with blood
> Drawn from Immanuel's veins,
> And sinners plunged beneath that flood
> Lose all their guilty stains.

Here is the fountain of youth! The future of the believer in Christ is ever young. As Psalm 48:14 promises, "For this God is our God for ever and ever; he will be our guide even to the end" and beyond.

The Rock of Ages Final Hall of Fame

The Baseball Hall of Fame is in Cooperstown, New York. The Football Hall of Fame is in Canton, Ohio. The Country Music Hall of Fame is in Nashville, Tennessee, and Cleveland has the Rock and Roll Hall of Fame.

But the Rock of Ages Hall of Fame is in heaven! How do we get selected for star status? Whom will God honor and approve?

He has given each of us a life to live with a set of abilities and opportunities. Someone said, "Only one life, 'twill soon be past, only what's done for God will last." But on our own, our efforts won't be enough to earn us heaven. That is why David said, "Do not bring your servant into judgment, for no one living is righteous before you" (Ps. 143:2).

Who do you think is the first one to enter into God's Hall of Fame? God set Jesus at His own right hand in the heavenly places that at the name of Jesus every knee shall bow. Yes, "Jesus Christ, Super Star" has the preeminence in all things.

This is true no matter what opinions people may hold of Him at present. When I was in the 8th grade, the teacher asked us to make our list of the ten greatest people in history. I put Jesus at the top. With annoyance, she crossed Him off. A lot she knew. God had already given Him the name above every name.

How did Christ earn first place, even though He was—and is—despised and rejected by many? He pleased not Himself, but gave Himself up for us all. He is the sacrifice for our sins. Thereby He purchased a place for you in the Rock of Ages Hall of Fame. It's yours for the asking.

To be included in the Rock of Ages Hall of Fame, you must aspire higher than the approval of mere humans. Reach for stardom by grasping hold of Jesus. Confess your sin and trust His redemption of your soul. Receive the Holy Spirit's power for a new life, enabling you to serve Christ and others the way He serves us.

The disciples of Christ were nobodies, but by faith in Jesus they became somebodies, and their names are written in the Lamb's book of life. That book is the Final and Forever Hall of Fame. By trusting in Christ, your name is inscribed there too.

God has the last word.

THOUGHTS OF HEAVEN

"I saw the Holy City..." Revelation 21:2

I'm taken up with thoughts of heaven,
I cannot put the subject down.
Living now in hour eleven,
The more I think such thoughts profound.

Am I prepared for such a vision,
And will it be as I've been told?
Will it be like Revelation,
With gates of pearl and streets of gold?

Walls of sapphire and sardonyx,
Topaz, emerald, and beryl;
With chrysoprase and amethyst,
Rich jacinth and jasper jewels?

Or will it be transcendent glory,
Earthly gems mere signs and symbols
Of much higher forms of beauty
Fitting for a place so royal?

As I read St. John's description,
I see so much of mystery
It almost makes one judge it fiction,
Instead of truthful prophecy.

But true it is and that verbatim.
We will see Christ as He is
And find ourselves exactly like Him.
What a splendid prospect this!

For eye has not seen, nor ear yet heard,
Nor has it occurred to our mind,
What God, our Savior, has prepared
For those who love Him—a grand design.

Family Forerunner

My youngest brother Lester was a happy boy. He loved God, his parents, six brothers, and one sister. At age four and a half, he was full of life and questions. As you might imagine, he was the "the apple of our eye."

Next door to the parsonage was a large church. As its tall spire dominated the flat farming landscape, its gospel message filled our lives and Lester's "with present joy and future hope." When we sat at the large kitchen table and had our family devotions, we could gaze out of three large windows across the back yard to the parish cemetery. How Lester loved to join in the songs around that table and listen to the Bible stories.

Then, after two days of scarlet fever he was gone, taken from our warm family circle in the spring of 1934.

Because several of us family members were still quarantined with scarlet fever, the funeral was held at the parsonage. The mourning congregation stood on the front lawn, the family sat in the living room, and the pastor-father ministered to both from the front porch doorway. We heard the resurrection victory of Jesus our Savior. We rejoiced that near the last Lester had sung, "Jesus loves me this I know." They carried our precious brother to the cemetery. We heard them sing and pray by the grave side in the sure hope of resurrection through Jesus Christ.

That evening at the kitchen table, in sight of the little grave, we reminisced over fond memories of Lester and shared the words of God that undergirded our hope in Jesus, the first-fruits of them that sleep. "For as in Adam all die, so in Christ all will be made alive" (1 Cor. 15:22). Because He died and rose again to cancel our debt of sin, we had the assurance of eternal life with the Lord in heaven.

Some families never speak of children who die young. Not so with us. Our parents always talked about Lester as though he still existed, because he did—in the loving care of God his Savior. Forty-one years later, when my mother left for the hospital in her last illness, she told my brother Vic, "I'm going to join Lester."

All of us recognize the spring of 1934 as the defining event of our family history. Lester's home going compelled us all to grasp the reality of the gospel and reaffirm our faith in Christ. In my own case, his death led me to my first attempts at poetry. On the next page are two poems I composed at age fourteen. The first I wrote originally in German and later translated into English.

THE SOUL OF THIS CHILD

The soul of this blossoming child
Is now so quickly taken away by angels
And carried so gently after he breathed his last.
This little saved, baptized child is now secure
And safe where there is no weeping and wailing,
But where praises and singing ring out.
And when we are united with him there,
We will all thank God and praise Him
In eternal adoration.

OUR COMFORT, OUR HOME IN HEAVEN

There is no home so greatly loved
As is that home in heaven above,
Nor is there any hope so true
Than that we'll reach that haven too.

Therefore, let's spread God's gospel well
To save the lost from sin and hell
Who have not seen the light to shine,
Nor heard those words of truth defined.

In Christ our faith should always lie.
There is no way to pass Him by.
For He's our Savior, God, and King
To Whom we owe just everything.

Our life and home we have from Him,
So let's with joyful voices sing
Our thanks to Christ, Who stood the pain
That we with Him in heaven might reign.

My Lifetime Fishing Buddy

I have a standing fishing appointment with my brother-in-law Frank Block.

Our fishing encounters began when I was courting his older sister. But then he went off to World War II. During those years he saw action in North Africa and Italy. Even now I vividly recall our thankfulness to God for his safe homecoming.

Upon his return in the spring of 1946, I invited him to go trout fishing. I wanted to introduce him to fly fishing which I had learned while he was in the service. What a fine time we had. Such a good time that Frank and I always made an appointment a year ahead to go fishing. Even after I moved to Ohio, we still met every year at Michigan's Au Sable River. What brought us back each year?

1. Our love of fly fishing. At first, I was the comparative expert, but Frank soon surpassed me. In fact, he became one of the best fishermen on the river. On nights when up and down the stream anglers like me were getting shut out, Frank would still be catching trout. I mean big ones!

2. Our friendship. We would catch up on what was happening in our lives, our work and our families. He had six children. I had five. There was always plenty to talk and laugh about.

3. Our faith. While we fished, it was as natural for us to share our convictions and love for the Lord, as our knowledge and love of fly fishing.

Frank went home to heaven in the spring of 1989, forty-three years after our first fly fishing jaunt. How I missed him during that fishing season.

But then I remembered that the preceding fall, Frank had given me a large trout he had just caught. I had put it in my freezer and forgotten all about it. As far as I know, it was the last fish he ever caught. So I took it to a taxidermist and had it mounted. Whenever I see that trout, I think of Frank, and I remember we have an appointment.

An appointment to meet where the river of life flows with water as clear as crystal. Frank, along with many other friends, and my Best Friend, Jesus, are my lifetime fishing buddies.

Share Christ with your fishing buddy, and you'll have one in heaven!

What Good Would Heaven Be without God?

"Whom have I in heaven but you? And earth has nothing I desire besides you." Psalm 73:25

What good would heaven be without God,
no matter how much else it offered?
To anticipate the glorious meeting
and then to find an empty house,
splendid mansion though it were.
To long for my Father's warm embrace
at the heavenly welcome-home party,
and find no Abba waiting there.

All that is splendid to please the eye,
celestial sounds to please the ear,
supernatural beauty and fragrance,
but no Rose of Sharon? No Jesus?!
A convocation of saved sinners,
a praise-gathering of souls in song,
an exultant "Glory be to Jesus,"
but the Son of God absent?

Angels, as eagles soaring free,
seraphim that wing-lift us above
to see the glory of the golden city,
but no sign of God's Spirit?
It would be a mere wilderness
causing thirst only God can quench.
The divine fountain but a desert mirage
now fading before our eyes.

In the splendid banquet hall
the wedding feast is now prepared.
The bride, the Church, gowned in white,
but no Bridegroom to be found?
All eyes search for His coming,
every ear strains for His footfall.
No bride ever so discarded,
no future ever so hollow.

No matter what wonders may appear,
heaven, without God, would barren be.
So great a vacuum would implode,

hope collapsed into despair.
"Oh, that I might see God", my soul would cry,
"to be home at last from wandering and wondering,
all love's yearning returned and satisfied
in Him from whom my whole life springs."

But God who cannot lie has promised.
When I awake, I will be with Him.
I will see Him as He is.
I will know Him as I am known.
He the center of my attention,
the sole object of my affection.
I shall be satisfied with His likeness.
My cup shall surely overflow. Forever.

These future musings instruct me now.
For is it not as true here as there?
Yes, He offers to reclaim my rebellious heart
and make my body His temple pure,
dwelling there as Comforter and Guide!
Here and now let us be heaven-minded,
filled with the fullness and presence of God,
our affection set on things above. Forever.

ETERNAL ATTENTION

Dear Father, tend me.
Jesus Savior, mend me.
Holy Spirit, bend me,
    send me,
    and spend me.
All Your power lend me.
Till the end defend me.
Then to heaven commend me.

TITLES LISTED ALPHABETICALLY

Agony and Ecstasy of Aging, The   114
Always the Same   31
Are You a Good Egg?   76
Augusta Vedra   116

Behold, the Goat of God   29
Bible Marking System   54
Biggest Fish Story Ever, The   13
Blood Cleanser   43

Caught by the Wrist   68
Christmas Mystery   51
Civil War II   110
Closing of the American Mind, The   109
Come!   42
Come, Pilgrim, Walk with Me   23
Continual Baptism   52

Easter—A New Dawn   33
Eternal Attention   124
"Evangelical" Is Our Middle Name   71
Every Soul Is Precious   64

Family Forerunner   120
Finders, Keepers   53
First Shall Be Last, The   52
First Thing on Jesus' Mind, The   63
For Deep Thirst   93
Fountain of Youth   117
Freeze!   72

Gifts Are for Sharing   56
God Be with You Till We Meet Again   90
Guard against the Interceptor   39
Guide to the Soul-Winner   74

Hear the Music in the Music of Xmas   24
He Is Our Life   46
His Banner over Us Is Love   107
Holy Land Morning   88
Holy Love   17
How Deep Is the Ocean?   94
How to Set a Church on Fire   60

Ignition   73
Improving Fishing Skills   80
I Must Speak   70
In Sync with God   98

Jesus Does the Laundry   34
Jesus Is the Key   36
Jesus, Rapture of My Heart   87

Key of Life, The   77

Lamb Is My Shepherd, The   96
Learning from the Master   11
Letter to Billy Graham, A   83
Life Billboards   46
Like a Drop of Water   58
Like Two Left Feet   103
Love that Never Fails   104

Martin Luther Describes the Soul-Winner   62
Marvelous Marriage Mathematics   102
Miracles! Miracles! Miracles!   34
My Lifetime Fishing Buddy   122

Names of Our Peace, The   44
Nearer Home   113
Needed: Prayer Warriors   92
New Verse to "His Name Is Wonderful"   38
New Verse to "You'll Never Walk Alone"   40
Normal Christian Lifestyle   69

O Lord, What a Morning!   94
Only Jesus   91
Our Christmas Hope   25
Our Comfort, Our Home in Heaven   121

Palm Sunday Psalm, A   28
Parachute, The   75
Poetry Defined   35
Praise God   93
Prayer for a Worshipful Spirit   86
Prayer for the Family   106
Precious Appreciation   103
Primary Election   108
Prisoner of War   22

Reason to Follow   100
Rock of Ages Hall of Fame, The   118

Second Wind for the Christian Walk   57
Short and Sweet Story, A   66
Soul of This Child, The   121
Soul-Winner's Prayer, A   67
Sunrise Sonrise   27
Sweet Harvest   84

Tested, Tempered, Triumphant   85
There Is a Way, America   111
Thoughts of Heaven   119
Tip for Fishers of Men, A   14

Very Personal   15

Wedding Benediction, A   101
We Have a Neat God   16
What Can Match Christ's Resurrection?   45
What Good Would Heaven Be without God?   123
What Grade Would You Give Jesus?   50
What I See by the Sea   99
What Is Jesus Like?   26
What Jesus Dreaded Most   30
Where Would I Go?   79
White and Gold Lily, The   32
Who Is the Rock   38
Whom Does God Choose?   41
With Jesus by the Sea   89
Witnessing in the Spirit   65
Witnessing May Take a Lifetime   18
Words in Tune   59

You'll See Adam before I Will   105

SCRIPTURE INDEX

Gen. 1:27   103

Lev. 16:7-10   29

Ps. 37:25   114
Ps. 42:1   93
Ps. 48:14   117
Ps. 51:10   35
Ps. 63:8   57
Ps. 73:25   123
Ps. 89:26   38
Ps. 92: 12. 14-15   115
Ps. 126   64
Ps. 143:2   118

Prov. 14:34   110, 111

Song of Songs 2:4   107

Is. 41:10   15
Is. 43:1   15
Is. 46:4   117
Is. 53:6   29, 66

Jer. 29:11   15
Jer. 31:3   15

Mt. 4:19   100
Mt. 11:30   76
Mt. 27:19   34
Mt. 27:45   34
Mt. 27: 51   34
Mt. 27:52   34
Mt. 27 66-28:4   34
Mt. 28:8   65
Mt. 28: 19   63

Mk. 1:35   94
Mk. 4:1-2   89
Mk. 7:37   50
Mk. 14:36   98
Mk. 15:38   34
Mk. 15:39   34

Lk. 1:46-47   25
Lk. 2:26, 27   51
Lk. 5:10   13

Lk. 22:8-38   34
Lk. 22:43   34
Lk. 22:44   30
Lk. 22:50-51   34
Lk. 23:34   34
Lk. 23:39-43   34
Lk. 24:48   63

Jn. 1:29   29
Jn. 3:16   15, 46
Jn. 3:30   14
Jn. 3:36   46, 75
Jn. 4:14   46
Jn. 5:24   46
Jn. 6:35, 40   47
Jn. 7:38   47
Jn. 8:12   16, 47
Jn. 8:36   78
Jn. 10:7, 8, 10, 11   47
Jn. 11:25   47
Jn. 11:43-44   34
Jn. 13:35   107
Jn. 14:2-3, 6   47
Jn. 14:6   111
Jn. 14:16   78
Jn. 14:19   75, 105
Jn. 15:13   107
Jn. 17:1-3   47
Jn. 18:4-6   34
Jn. 19:30   50
Jn. 20:21   63
Jn. 21:15, 17   63

Acts 1:8   63
Acts 2   69
Acts 2:38   66
Acts 4:20   70
Acts 16:31   66
Acts 26: 2   74

Rom. 3:23   66
Rom. 6:4   57
Rom. 6:23   66, 115
Rom. 7 & 8   36
Rom. 8:4   57
Rom. 13:13   57

1 Cor. 15:22   120
1 Cor. 15:54   45
1 Cor. 15:55, 57   78

2 Cor. 4:4   110

Gal. 3:27   75
Gal. 5:16   57

Eph. 3:19   94
Eph. 2:10   57, 59
Eph. 4:12   57
Eph. 5:15   57
Eph. 5:25-27   35, 104
Eph. 6:12, 18a   92

Phil. 4: 13, 19   58
Col. 1:10   57
Col. 2:6   57
Col. 2:9-10   50
Col. 4:5   57

1 Thes. 2:12   57

2 Tim. 1:10   78, 117

Heb. 2:14   78
Heb. 9:22   43
Heb. 10:14   50
Heb. 12:2   35

Jas. 2:10   66
Jas. 5:8   15

1 Jn. 1:5   16
1 Jn. 1:7   43, 66, 104
1 Jn. 3:1   104
1 Jn. 4:7   17

3 Jn. 1:4   106

Rev. 1:18   36, 77
Rev. 7:9, 14   35, 43
Rev. 7:17   95
Rev. 15:4   17
Rev. 21:2   119

About Roller Coaster Press

Dr. Philip M. Bickel founded Roller Coaster Press in 1998 to facilitate the publication of evangelism and mission resources. He has served as a church planter, missionary to Venezuela, writer/producer of a Spanish media ministry, evangelism pastor, professor of Christian outreach, and missions pastor. Phil earned the M. Div. at Concordia, Springfield, IL, and the D. Missiology at Trinity, Deerfield, IL. Here are some titles by Dr. Bickel which are available through Roller Coaster Press.

Outreach Promises:
God's Encouragement for Sharing Your Faith

The Lord never intended to burden you with witnessing guilt and fears. Instead, He peppered the Bible with outreach promises to lift your sights and renew your vision for the lost. Find out how to identify and apply these promises to your life. Includes a Group Discussion Guide. ISBN 0-9663765-0-1 112 pp. $8.95

New Creeds for Today's Needs:
Giving a Relevant Witness to Contemporary Issues

Recognize modern questions in need of new, biblical responses. Follow step-by-step methods for "creed teams" to design new confessions in any medium.they desire to use. Includes an example of a new creed responding to spiritism. 24 pp. $2.95

The Goal of the Gospel:
God's Purpose in Saving You

God saved and equipped you for a purpose. Have you discovered it? An eye-opening view of Romans as Paul the Missionary intended it to be understood. Ideal for lay Bible studies. Co-author: Robert L. Nordlie. ISBN 0-570-04569-X 272 pp. $14.95

Considering a Church Career?:
Determining God's Plan for Your Life

Need career counseling about church work? Here it is. Answers questions commonly asked by youth and adults seeking God's will. Directs you from the "just toying" stage to concrete actions. Co-author: Curtis Deterding. ISBN 0-570-04850-8 64 pp. $3.50

Learn more about these and other titles at: http://www.christianlink.com/evangelism/encourager. Phil Bickel also is available to speak and teach. E-mail: pmbickel@aol.com. Phone: 888-894-1594. Mail: 1167 Ryan Avenue W., Roseville, MN 55113-5929.

ORDER FORM

You may return undamaged items for a refund, within 1 year.
For multiple orders, please photocopy this form.
All orders must be prepaid.

Name: _____ Tel.: _____

Address: _____ Fax: _____

City: _____ E-mail: _____

State/Province: _____ Postal Code: _____ Country: _____

Ship to (if different than above):

Name: _____ Tel.: _____

Address: _____ Fax: _____

City: _____ E-mail: _____

State/Province: _____ Postal Code: _____ Country: _____

Please send the following items: (*Circle the appropriate price.*)

TITLES	RETAIL(1-2)	DISCOUNT(3+)	QTY.		AMOUNT
Fishing for Souls	$14.99	$11.99	x ____	=	$_____
Outreach Promises	$ 8.95	$ 5.37	x ____	=	$_____
New Creeds for Today's Needs	$ 2.95	$ 2.35	x ____	=	$_____
The Goal of the Gospel	$14.95	$11.95	x ____	=	$_____
Considering a Church Career?	$ 3.50	$ 2.95	x ____	=	$_____
			Sub-total:		$_____
Add 6.5% sales tax for shipments to Minnesota:					$_____
		Add shipping/handling:			$ 3.50
			TOTAL:		$_____

Make check or money order payable to: Roller Coaster Press.

    On-line orders: pmbickel@aol.com
    Telephone orders: 888-894-1594
    Mail orders: Roller Coaster Press
                  1167 Ryan Avenue West
                  Roseville, MN 55113-5929

Contact Roller Coaster Press for savings on large quantity orders.